ON BMW

1981-1986

Reprinted From
Cycle World Magazine

ISBN 1 869826 566

Published By
Brooklands Books with permission of Cycle World

Titles in this series

CYCLE WORLD ON BMW 1964-1973
CYCLE WORLD ON BMW 1974-1980
CYCLE WORLD ON BMW 1981-1986
CYCLE WORLD ON BSA 1962-1971
CYCLE WORLD ON DUCATI 1962-1980
CYCLE WORLD ON DUCATI 1982-1991
CYCLE WORLD ON HARLEY-DAVIDSON 1962-1968
CYCLE WORLD ON HARLEY-DAVIDSON 1968-1978
CYCLE WORLD ON HARLEY-DAVIDSON 1978-1983
CYCLE WORLD ON HARLEY-DAVIDSON 1983-1987
CYCLE WORLD ON HARLEY-DAVIDSON 1987-1990
CYCLE WORLD ON HARLEY-DAVIDSON 1990-1992
CYCLE WORLD ON HONDA 1962-1967
CYCLE WORLD ON HONDA 1968-1971
CYCLE WORLD ON HONDA 1971-1974
CYCLE WORLD ON HUSQVANA 1966-1976
CYCLE WORLD ON HUSQVANA 1977-1984
CYCLE WORLD ON KAWASAKI 1966-1971
CYCLE WORLD ON KAWASAKI OFF-ROAD BIKES 1972-1976
CYCLE WORLD ON KAWASAKI STREET BIKES 1972-1976
CYCLE WORLD ON NORTON 1962-1971
CYCLE WORLD ON TRIUMPH 1962-1967
CYCLE WORLD ON TRIUMPH 1967-1972
CYCLE WORLD ON TRIUMPH 1972-1987
CYCLE WORLD ON SUZUKI 1967-1970
CYCLE WORLD ON SUZUKI OFF-ROAD BIKES 1971-1976
CYCLE WORLD ON SUZUKI STREET BIKES 1971-1976
CYCLE WORLD ON YAMAHA 1962-1969
CYCLE WORLD ON YAMAHA OFF-ROAD BIKES 1970-1974
CYCLE WORLD ON YAMAHA STREET BIKES 1970-1974

DISTRIBUTED BY

CarTech,
11481 Kost Dam Road,
North Branch,
MN 55056, USA
Phone: 800 551 4754 & 612 583 3471
Fax: 612 583 2023

Brooklands Books Ltd.,
1/81 Darley St.,
PO Box 199, Mona Vale,
NSW 2103, Australia
Phone: 2 997 8428
Fax: 2 452 4679

Brooklands Books Ltd,
PO Box 146,
Cobham, Surrey KT11 1LG
England
Phone: 0932 865051
Fax: 0932 868803

Printed in Hong Kong

CYCLE WORLD

5	BMW for 1981	*Cycle World*	Jan.	1981
6	BMW R80G/S Road Test	*Cycle World*	April	1981
14	BMW R100CS Road Test	*Cycle World*	August	1981
21	BMW R100RS/F.	*Cycle World*	April	1982
24	BMW R65LS Road Test	*Cycle World*	March	1982
31	BMW News	*Cycle World*	April	1982
32	BMW R80ST Road Test	*Cycle World*	Oct.	1983
38	A Four Like No Other	*Cycle World*	Jan.	1984
42	A Bold New Wager Against the Virtues of Tradition	*Cycle World*	Sept.	1984
50	Good as Gold	*Cycle World*	Jan.	1985
54	BMW K100RT Road Test	*Cycle World*	April	1985
60	BMW R80RT Road Test	*Cycle World*	Oct.	1985
66	Distant Riders	*Cycle World*	Nov.	1985
72	BMW K75 Riding Impressions	*Cycle World*	Dec.	1985
74	BMW K75C Road Test	*Cycle World*	April	1986
80	BMW K75S Riding Impression	*Cycle World*	Dec.	1986

We are frequently asked for copies of out of print Road Tests and other articles that have appeared in Cycle World. To satisfy this need we are producing a series of books that will include, as nearly as possible, all the important information on one make or subject for a given period.

It is our hope that these collections of articles will give an overview that will be of value to historians, restorers and potential buyers, as well as to present owners of these interesting motorcycles.

BMW for 1981
An 800cc Dual Purpose Twin Heads the List
by Ron Griewe

BMW is a company that forges ahead in a slow and normally cautious manner. Radical design concepts, styling or mechanical, are usually shunned in favor of gradual refinement of the Boxer Twin born in the early Thirties. But, when BMW does make a radical design decision, they like to make the introduction an event to remember.

This one began with an invitation from BMW motorcycle manager Rolf Kettler. Would someone from *CW* like to attend an international press introduction of BMW's new R80G/S off-road bike? The event was in the south of France and maybe we would be interested in a two day ride from southern France through the French and Swiss Alps to Munich, Germany after the R80G/S intro?

Of course, we were interested! Wow, a dirt bike from BMW. Would it be a replica of the bike BMW has been running in the ISDT for the past couple of years?

BMW officials met us at the Frankfort airport and after a night at a beautiful old hotel we boarded another plane for the short ride to southern France. A double deck bus took us from Nimes to Avigon and another four-star hotel with a nine course dinner in the Ancient Pope's Palace.

After formal introductions of the BMW corporate people, the GS80 intro got into full swing. The chief engineer explained the design and the intended use of the R80G/S. No, it isn't a full-blown dirt machine. It's the world's largest dual purpose bike. And a dual purpose machine from BMW makes more sense than an all-out cross country racer. Most European countries don't have areas of vacant land open for cross country riding. But virtually all the dirt roads leading into the forests are open for use. Thus it's a trail bike that's a good highway cruiser.

THE R80G/S

The 80G/S is more than a street bike with dirt tires. The GS has its own R65-derived frame with a single rear shock. The single shock is placed on the right side of the machine in a canted forward position. The shock is gas charged but doesn't have a remote reservoir. The shock body is the same size as that used on dual shock applications so oil capacity is small and overheating and fading result if extended rough cross country terrain is crossed.

With the single shock mounted to the right side of the swing arm, there's not much need for the other side of the arm, and BMW has eliminated it. BMW claims 4.4 lb. is saved by leaving off the second shock and left side of the swing arm, yet increased torsional stability of the arm by 40 percent. Shaft drive from the street BMs has been retained in the interest of reliability and maintenance. The drive shaft uses the swing arm for a housing and the differential bolts to it. The 3.36:1 final drive ratio is slightly lower than BMW's large street Twins, in the interest of low speed response. A drum rear brake is used, a single drilled disc brake is standard at the front. Both wheels use normal wire spokes, because they are lighter than cast wheels and allow some flex to prevent breakage.

The single shock, single swing arm seems like a radical departure from the normal and is. It has some definite advantages. Tire repair or replacement is a breeze; just heft the bike onto its center stand and remove the tire. With no swing arm in the way, there's no reason to remove the wheel, hence, no drive or brake linkage to unhook. If the wheel does need removing for some reason, it's a simple job. Three nuts hold it on and the tool kit contains a small lug wrench especially for the job. Tire tools are also in the tool kit and an air pump is stored in the frame's backbone.

Forks are BMW built units with rubber gaiters. They are almost the same as those used on the BMW R65 and have 7.8 in. of travel. Rear wheel travel is 6.7 in. Dual purpose tires are designed and built by Metzeler for the R80G/S. The knob pattern is different from any we have seen before. The knobs are short and triangular. The profile is a rounded shape, more like a street tire than dirt, although the tires perform fairly well on both surfaces. The design is certified safe to speeds of 111 mph (180 km/h). The R80 will only do about 105 mph so an owner need not worry about exceeding the safe limit of the tires when on paved surfaces.

The 800cc engine, largest ever for a dual purpose machine, has been modernized. CD ignition is standard and both electric and kick start are used. A new dry clutch with diaphragm spring and lightweight flywheel are furnished. Clutch pull at the lever is 40 percent easier, engagement is more progressive and control is improved. The flywheel is 8 lb. lighter than before. Cylinders are new, with steel-aluminum bores. This change was made to reduce cylinder weight and to reduce oil consumption. Piston clearance can be about 30 percent tighter and the bore doesn't distort as badly when hot. But replacement of the cylinders is necessary if damaged or worn as they can't be rebored.

The R80G/S has a 2-into-1 exhaust system. Both headpipes turn and roll under the cylinders, coming together at the left rear of the engine where they enter the single high mounted silencer. The large silencer looks heavy but the nice quiet sound it emits makes it all worthwhile.

Several parts of the R80 are fiberglass. Both side panels are hand-laid glass, as is the seat base. The prototype fiberglass parts on the press bikes were fragile and half of the bikes were missing side covers by the end of the day. BMW personnel assured us the production parts would be much stronger but . . . plastic pieces would be better. Both fenders and the headlight housing are made from plastic and can't be faulted. The steel fuel tank holds 5.1 gal. of gasoline. Or about 30 lb. of it. Added to the R80's dry weight of 365 lb. a dirt rider has to wrestle 400 lb. of motorcycle.

Viewed as a dual purpose machine, and BMW doesn't claim the bike to be anything but dual purpose, the bike will probably be fine. For the person who wants to

CONTINUED ON PAGE 13

BMW R80 G/S

CYCLE WORLD TEST

■ Some motorcycle companies offer 50 or more models every year, with engines that are 50 to 1100cc, two–strokes and four, in a selection including mopeds, motocrossers, city scooters, sports racers and fully-equipped touring mounts.

Some motorcycle companies specialize and one of the best-known for this has been BMW. For the past generation BMW has offered what amounts to one engine in a variety of sizes and one usage, the highway. There have been some exceptions, for example the ISDT specials BMW runs once each year but in general, ever since the invention of the pure dirt bike, BMW has not offered anything that didn't have pavement written under it.

Surprise. Late in 1980 BMW introduced something different. Not quite new, as the R80 G/S (the initials stand for Woods/Street in German) uses the familiar R80 opposed Twin. Not really dirt, because those ISDT bikes are conventional racers, rather than new ideas. Not exactly dual purpose as the 80 G/S isn't as light as the standard dual-purpose Singles and isn't really intended for actual rock-bashing and mud-crawling.

Different. What BMW has in mind is the explorer market, or maybe the adventure market. The 80 G/S is supposed to be a go-anywhere motorcycle, for riders who want to cross Tunisia or go from Alaska to the tip of South America. The G/S has extra ground clearance, special tires, a rear suspension that's different in a model year when single rear shocks are more common than not. To keep costs and prices down, most of the G/S is shared with other BMWs. That means it's easier to bring out the different model than it would be to begin making an entirely new engine and drivetrain.

Because BMW clearly says that the G/S is not a dirt bike or a conventional dual-purpose bike or touring bike, we

Photos by Ron Brewer

Not a Lightweight Street Bike. Surely Not a Heavyweight ISDT Mount. Instead, It's a Bike for Exploring.

didn't give it the conventional test. The western equivalent of Africa or the Alps or South America is Baja California, the isolated peninsula below American California and west of the Mexican mainland. Roads are tricky and unmarked, gas stations are widely spaced and motorcycle stores aren't there at all. Baja scenery is beautiful and for those who can tackle dirt roads and trails there are scores of things to see, from 200-year-old missions to whales in love. Thus, we asked for two R80s and prepared to explore.

But first, more about the machine. The G/S frame is normal BMW in the front, with widely separated downtubes that run beneath the engine then curve back up to join the single backbone. The steering head junctions are reinforced with gussets and extra tubes. The rear subframe is new and different. In effect it holds up the seat and extends beneath the seat only on the right, where the frame meets the upper end of the single rear shock. The lower shock mount is half a swing arm that also houses the drive shaft. This looks very different and draws questions about how strong half a swing arm can be.

Hell for strong, the BMW engineers say. Their lab tests show the single leg and mounting point provide 30 percent more torsional rigidity while reducing weight, unsprung weight at that, by nearly 5 lb.

We can't argue with that. The rider quickly forgets that the arrangement is different. There's no feeling of flex or of imbalance.

Except maybe when you look at the left side of the G/S. There's nothing there. The frame and drivetrain stop and there's just a wheel, running all the way around.

This has an advantage all its own. Nothing is in the way when working from the left side of the bike. If there is a need to remove the wheel, it's a simple job. The rear wheel mounts like no other motorcycle wheel—with three automobile type lug nuts. The excellent tool kit contains a lug wrench for the purpose. It has to be the easiest rear wheel ever to remove.

The G/S front is something of an evolu- >

tion. The forks are similar to those introduced on the R65. They have more control than the forks on the larger Bimmers, which reduces the softness and excessive pitch under braking of the older models. Front wheel travel for the G/S is 8 in., nearly a dirt bike dimension. The wheel is a 21-incher, also dirt style and the tire is a new dual purpose pattern, a Metzeler design done just for this bike although it will be sold as a replacement for other brands and models. Interesting tread, with pentagonal knobs where the traditional Dunlop and Pirelli universals have square knobs. (The 18-in. rear tire has the same pattern.)

All the larger BMWs will use the new forks for 1981. Spring and damping rates, according to BMW, are unchanged for the 1000cc BMWs using these new leading axle forks. The same sort of sharing involves engine components, such as the all-aluminum cylinders. They have a high silicon content and the working surfaces of the bores are coated with nickel. Heat conductivity is three times better than before, which allows closer piston clearances. That in turn shortens break-in time and reduces oil consumption. As a bonus, the new cylinders are more than 6 lb. lighter than the old ones.

The points and coil ignition has been replaced by an electronic system, the flywheel is 8 lb. lighter and the dry, single-plate clutch is lighter and has a diaphragm spring that reduces effort at the clutch lever.

The G/S exhaust system is designed for off-road use. The headpipes roll under the cylinders, joining at the rear of the cases before they enter the left side high mounted silencer. Although the headpipes are tucked in tightly, they could use a crash guard or skid plate to protect against rocks and such.

Footpegs, shift lever and rear brake pedal are made especially for the G/S. The pegs are folding motocross designs with saw-toothed tops and strong return springs. The stamped steel shift lever pivots on the frame and connects to the transmission via linkage. It looks strange in its reversed position; the pivot in front, the shift rubber end to the rear. The brake pedal also has a saw-toothed foot surface. Neither lever folds but then it's not as necessary on the BMW because both are somewhat protected (!) by the protruding cylinders.

Fuel tank capacity is a whopping 5.1 gal. Only one petcock is used, on the left side. It is a simple down for on, sideways for off, and up for reserve.

The 80G/S has its own orange colored seat. The base is plastic and the foam is thicker than that used on the street versions. But we'll talk about the comfort later in the test. It's quickly removable from the bike by simply pushing a button at the back. The button is fitted with a key lock to prevent unwanted removal and

Removing the engine covers is a simple job; four allen head screws gets it down to this point. Standard kick start pedal is retained for emergencies.

keeps thieves from the excellent tool kit that rests in a tray under the seat. A tire pump comes with each G/S and is neatly stored in the frame's backbone tube. A nice German cold patch kit is also packed in the tool kit tray, so flats won't pose much of a problem for the G/S rider.

Instrumentation consists of a pod that surrounds the quartz-halogen headlight and holds the speedometer, a panel of warning lights for the signals, oil pressure, neutral, alternator and high beam, and the ignition—the fork lock is separate—switch. It's a neat enough collection, although having green for turn signals and green for neutral can be confusing. The G/S doesn't get signal beepers, hurray. The odometer has a push-button reset which looks useful but first, the rubber cover fell off and rain water leaked inside and didn't dry out for three days, second the push sometimes stuck on zero and needed jiggling to restart.

Because the adventure bike is intended for a variety of uses it's offered with a long list of options. You can get different final drive ratios, a side stand—more about *that* later—a rear shock with reservoir, a luggage rack for the rear fender and a solo saddlebag for the right side only. The factory could only supply one bag and one rack, so the local dealer fitted our second G/S with an aftermarket rack. It was higher than the BMW item, and looked, uh, as if it had been added at the last minute, but it worked.

The saddlebag is the BMW unit sold for other models so it's shaped to clear a shock and it goes on the right. Odd, in that if they used the left side, they could have a larger bag. But then the high-mounted muffler might get in the way. The bag will open and close without locking and snaps on and off the brackets without the key also, so it's quick and easy. The tongue for

the lock attaches to the bracket with two visible bolts: a thief would not be deterred.

With 648 mi. on one bike and 1058 mi. on the other, we packed up and headed for Baja. The plan was to head down the freeway to the Mexican border, a mere 100 mi. from our offices, get Mexican insurance, then head south to the end of available

BMW's version of a single shock, shaft drive motorcycle uses a single arm. Rear tire and wheel service is easy with no swing arm in the way. High mounted silencer is quiet but needs a heat shield to prevent burning articles stored on the rear of the bike.

land, a place called Cabo San Lucas. We figured eight to 10 days would give us time to effectively evaluate the bike in surroundings it was designed for. Baja has only one paved road that goes to the end of the peninsula, Mexican Hwy 1. It meanders around, starting on the Pacific Ocean side of Tijuana, then crossing the narrow land mass about half way down, running on the Gulf of California through Santa Rosalia, Mulege and Loreto before swinging back to the middle of the peninsula for a couple hundred miles, then turning back to the Gulf at La Paz. From La Paz it's only 140 mi. to the tip at Cabo San Lucas. Baja's paved roads are poorly paved and poorly maintained. The original pavement, put down five years ago, wasn't very thick. Overloaded Mexican trucks and extreme winters have made many sections rougher than dirt roads; encountering a section of nasty chuckholes at speed is common, and of course, there's no warning. Also, some interesting places can be >

explored by venturing down the rock and dirt roads in Baja.

Two hundred year old missions, neat little ranches nestled in green valleys and beautiful white beaches that're completely deserted are available to the curious. Perfect for an adventure bike.

Cruising down the Interstates and maintained highways reminded us once again of just how nice a lightweight road bike and a big Twin can be. The Metzeler universals were quiet, the engine just lazed along in top gear with nothing except an authoritative low-frequency shake to remind the rider that the engine is booming out the miles. Before we began, we wondered how having one saddle bag would affect the handling. Before we reached the border we'd not only forgotten to worry, we'd forgotten the bag was there.

Shifting is much improved with the new clutch and lighter flywheel; no clunk or clank, but there is a tendency to hang up between gears. The shift throw is long and combined with the hitch in the middle of each shift, takes a little getting used to. Otherwise a neutral pops up. The shift from neutral to first feels sticky and the tranny doesn't always go into low with the first prod. Both problems had almost disappeared by the test's end, though.

Both brakes also take time to seat before becoming fully effective. After a couple of thousand miles both start working smoothly and need less force to operate. The front still requires more muscle than comparable Japanese discs, but not nearly as much as the older BMWs. And the unit is strong enough to slide the front tire on paved surfaces.

Twisty sections of secondary pavement are pure pleasure on the G/S. It zips in and out of corners like the lightweight street bike it is. Nothing drags or grinds itself away; cornering speeds are determined by the rider, not the bike's exterior parts. Directional control is excellent. The GS goes where it's pointed, no hassle or head of its own. The bike is an extension of the rider.

The handlebars are, naturally, a compromise. They fit dirt use fine; on the street they are okay at low speeds but the straight up riding position they dictate lets the wind buffet the rider at higher speeds. The blast of wind on the rider's chest also causes arm ache and fatigue at an accelerated rate. A small quarter fairing and slightly lower bars would help the bike's high speed comfort a bunch and wouldn't bother the dirt use enough to matter.

Other on-road handling is normal BMW. The bike doesn't dart around on grooved pavement and the tall top gear ratios let the engine almost idle at posted highway speeds. And engine sounds almost disappear completely; no whine, buzz or other annoyances. The rider can sit back and enjoy the scenery without distraction.

In-town riding takes a little getting used to. The abundance of torque at low engine speeds makes the shift from low to second touchy. A normal shift and clutch release will cause a leap ahead. Winding the engine in low a little and slowing the clutch release smoothes the shift. It just takes a little practice.

Keeping with the explorer theme we ventured off the pavement and up various dirt roads on the way down the peninsula. Dirt suits the G/S right down to the semi-knobbies. Assuming the rider remembers it isn't a YZ465 or an XR750, that is, assuming speeds are held down and a hazard around the next curve is expected, the G/S works quite well. Rocks make the bike's weight felt and one never forgets those cylinders sticking 'way out. We never actually bashed one but we did have a spare rocker cover along just in case we forgot that the G/S is the world's widest dual-purpose bike.

In sand, the G/S was not as good. Better than a road bike, but not good. The front is simply too heavy and the 3.00 section tire knifes for the bottom while the long frame and short swing arm set up a wobble.

Sliding a dirt turn with the GS is, well, different. The cylinders are right where your foot should go. Thus, the rider has to put his foot behind the cylinder, loading the bike too far to the rear. The rear loading and short swing arm cause severe sawing through the corner. Best to forget about putting your foot down in corners; the bike will saw less and better control is maintained. Putting your foot down on a bike that weighs over 400 lb. isn't going to do much anyway, unless you're a professional football tackle.

Suspension is pretty good for a dual purpose bike. The single shock rear works better than the front. The rear soaks up bumps and holes well until the limits of its travel are reached, then naturally bottoms, but not hard. The forks aren't as comfortable. They transmit some shock to the rider, don't bottom harshly, but do top anytime the front wheel leaves the ground. The topping is constant when the bike is ridden in the dirt, especially if the ground is littered with rocks. Drilling a bigger hole in the top of the damper rod would probably cure the topping; too bad the factory didn't do it.

The orange seat that looks so comfortable is pure torture for long rides. Fifty miles at a sitting is the limit. And the second 50 gets longer. After a couple of days in the saddle, moving around constantly, trying to find a spot or position that's comfortable takes a lot of the fun out of riding the bike. Three days into the trip, (1200 mi.), we couldn't stand sitting on the seat any longer and decided to spend a day in La Paz. Lying in the sun and walking around town brought the feeling back to our butts. Heading back we made about 75 mi. before the ache was back. After that we vowed to stop and rest at 50 mi.

Dual purpose Metzeler tires are good all around tires. Bike is fairly narrow except for the cylinders.

intervals no matter where we were. A $4800 bike deserves a better seat—much better.

Hand controls took some getting used to. BMW has adopted the left-right turn switch, as opposed to the old up-down system and we approve of that. But on the G/S the horn button, dimmer switch and turn switch are bunched together, a good reach from the left grip. A gloved finger can't quite fit between any two and it was all too common at first for the intended turn signal to emerge as a flash of the brights at some innocent oncomer or the car just ahead. Or the horn button doesn't get found—you dare not look for it—until the hazard is past. The dog-legged anodized levers are fine and the grips are normal cone-shaped BMW rubber, as in some like 'em, some don't.

The gear-drive, straight-pull throttle keeps the cable tucked out of harm's way but the effort to work it seems a bit much for only two CV carbs. The G/S doesn't come with the optional set-screw but the housing is tapped for it, so we had the screws installed on both test bikes. Good for highway cruising but awkward in town until you remember to back off the tension.

Oh, yeah, the stand. Every test since the invention of the boxer Twin has griped about the BMW snap-up sidestand, the one that retracts as soon as you want, if not before. So for 1981 BMW has gone to a stand that isn't hidden when up and that locks when down.

And for the G/S, the side stand is an option. What you get standard is a center stand that hides itself when up. When lowered the stand's outboard peg is clever- >

BMW R80 G/S

SPECIFICATIONS

List price $4800
Engine ......ohv opposed Twin
Bore x stroke 84.8 x 70.6mm
Displacement 797.5cc
Compression ratio.......8.2:1
Carburetion........ (2) 32mm
Bing CV
Air filter ....treated paper
Ignition ....electronic
Claimed power ....na
Claimed torque ....na
Lubrication ....wet sump
Oil capacity ....2.4 qt.
Fuel capacity ....5.1 gal.
Starter ....electric, kick
Electrical power..........280w
alternator
Battery ....12v / 12ah
Headlight ....60 / 55w halogen
Primary drive..............shaft
Clutch ....dry, single plate
Final drive ....shaft
Gear ratios, overall:1
5th 5.04
4th 5.61
3rd 6.96
2nd 9.61
1st 14.78
Suspension:
Front ....telescopic fork
travel ....8.0 in.
Rear..............swing arm
travel ....7.0 in.
Tires:
Front................ 3.00-21
Metzeler Enduro
Rear................. 4.00-18
Metzeler Enduro
Brakes:
Front............10.2 in. disc
Rear......single 7.9 in. disc
Brake swept area ..104 sq. in.
Brake loading (160-lb.
rider) ....5.74 lb. / sq. in.
Wheelbase ....57.7 in.
Rake / Trail.......27.5° / 4.5 in.
Handlebar width ......31.3 in.
Seat height ....33.6 in.
Seat width ....7.1 in.
Footpeg height........13.6 in.
Ground clearance ......8.0 in.
Test weight
(w / half-tank fuel) ..437 lb.
Weight bias,
% front / rear .....45.3 / 54.7
GVWR ....878 lb.
Load capacity ....441 lb.

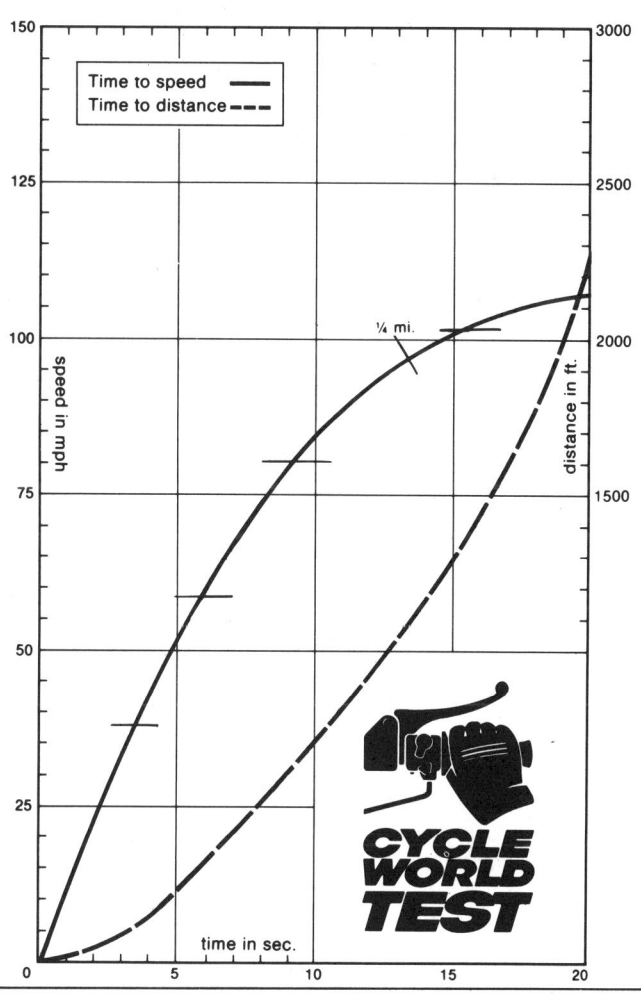

Time to speed ———
Time to distance ----

speed in mph

distance in ft.

¼ mi.

time in sec.

CYCLE
WORLD
TEST

PERFORMANCE

Standing ¼-mile....13.80 sec.
@ 94.53 mph
Top speed in ½-mile .105 mph
Fuel consumption......51 mpg
Range (to reserve) ...230 mi.
Acceleration:
0–30 mph......... 2.0 sec.
0–40 mph......... 3.1 sec.
0–50 mph......... 4.3 sec.
0–60 mph......... 6.0 sec.
0–70 mph......... 7.2 sec.
0–80 mph......... 9.3 sec.
0–90 mph......... 12.3 sec.
0–100 mph ....17.5 sec.
Top gear acceleration:
40–60 mph........ 6.3 sec.
60–80 mph ....6.3 sec.
Maximum speed in gears:
1st.................. 37 mph
2nd.................. 57 mph
3rd.................. 79 mph
4th.................. 98 mph
5th..................109 mph
Speedometer error:
30 mph indicated 28.35 mph
60 mph indicated 57.91 mph
Braking distance:
from 30 mph.......... 36 ft.
from 60 mph........ 159 ft.
Engine speed
at 60 mph 4055

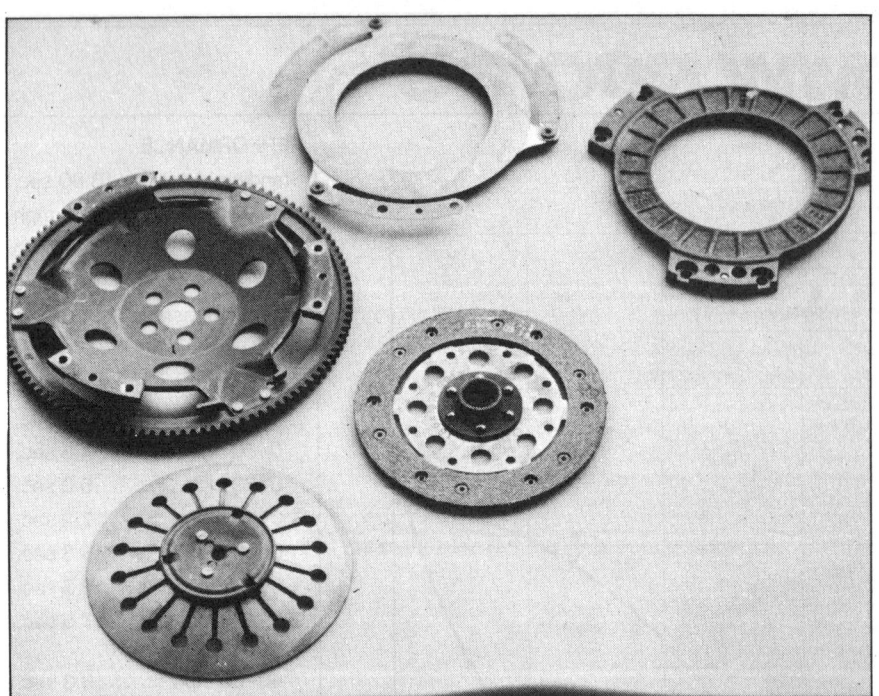

New instrument pod has the normal assortment of lights. High beam light is excessively bright and distracts the rider. Speedo reset is accomplished by pushing the button on the bottom of the dial. Water readily entered one of the units.

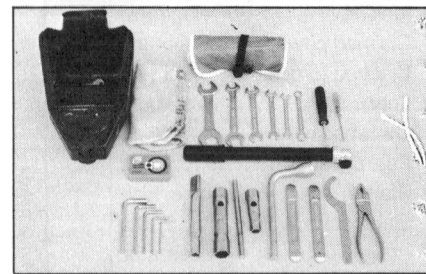

Excellent tool kit contains a complete wrench set, air pump, spanner wrench, patch kit, grease rag, pliers, allen head wrenches, screw drivers sockets and lug wrench.

New clutch and flywheel are 8 lb. lighter. Clutch pull is light and doesn't slip. Lighter unit makes for more responsive engine and better shifting.

ly placed exactly inboard of the left peg. The one with teeth on it. Step down and pull up in the usual way and you get the peg snapped into your shin. Only way it works is to put the sole of your right boot on the back of the stand, cock your leg behind the peg and pull, haul and pivot all in one motion. Leaning the bike against a tree is easier. We haven't tried the optional side stand, but it's got to be worth whatever it costs.

We were gone long enough to ride the G/S in all kinds of weather. It blows around in side winds and meeting large trucks on narrow roads is quite a thrill; it darts around like a wounded guppy. Muddy roads are handled with much better control than one would have with a pure street bike and street only tires. Wet roads pose no problem; the tires grip well on wet surfaces. Tire wear is rapid. With 3000 mi. on the bikes the rear tire was worn smooth.

Baja is a great place for road hazard surprises. Most danger spots are unmarked and roadracing into a sweeper at 80 plus can cause fear for the body. One such corner turned to pea gravel part way through, no warning of course. The G/S did some heavy duty sliding and shuddering but didn't go down or off the road. It could have been a grim situation with road tires and a softly sprung suspension.

Gas mileage of the G/S won't win any awards. It produced 51 mpg on our mileage loop but only averaged 35 mpg during the Baja trip. But then we rode harder while in Baja and fuel quality was marginal.

After 2400 mi. of Baja, both on and off-road, we have to rate the GS80 as a worth-

while design. It doesn't work as well off-road as we'd like but will get the job done if ridden carefully. It's better off-road than any other 800cc bike we can think of.

Problems were few; the leaky speedo on one bike we already talked about, the Bing carburetors on both bikes started leaking with the engine off, and one carb leaked slightly the whole trip, running or not. One bike decided it didn't want to start in gear, requiring the rider to search for neutral before starting each time. The poor quality Mexican gas caused considerable pinging if the engines were bogged but it didn't create a big problem. Still, a bike designed for back country use should have a little lower compression ratio so pinging wouldn't be a problem with low octane fuel. The new aluminum cylinders have cured the oil using problems of past BMWs. Each bike covered the 2400 mi. without needing oil. Both burned less than a quarter of a quart. The new clutch

makes pulling the clutch lever much easier and there's no more clutch slip or noise when power shifting. And we didn't burn it up at the drag strip like many past BMW clutches.

Engine performance isn't breathtaking, in fact the bike is rather slow for an 800. Quarter mile times were in the high 13s with terminal speeds around 94 mph. Top speed after a half mile was 105 mph. Braking distances were a little disappointing also. The narrow rear tire slides and goes up in smoke easily during panic stops.

With the 80G/S long trips through countries with marginal or almost no road, are suddenly possible. And the high speed freeways or autobahns on the way won't intimidate the bike. Almost any trip can be made with the confidence the bike will endure. All in all, the 80 G/S is a great machine for getting away from it all. Wonder how long a trip from the tip of South America to California would take? ◘

Shift linkage on the G/S is unusual.

CONTINUED FROM PAGE 5

ride on the street most of the time but likes to stray down an occasional dirt road or trail at moderate speeds, or the person who rides many twisty secondary paved roads, the R80G/S could be a logical choice. The R80 excels on curved roads. A 400 lb. 800cc street machine is a lightweight. And the lighter flywheel and new clutch make the R80 an agile and responsive canyon racer. Shifting the five-speed transmission is easy and positive and using the clutch isn't necessary. BMW credits the new ease of shifting to the lighter flywheel, claiming the transmission is unchanged. The dual purpose tires limit cornering speeds on the street but aren't too bad. In the dirt they don't grip like full knobbies but again aren't too bad. Sliding dirt roads is usually great fun on a four-stroke dirt bike but the R80 doesn't adapt to it. The short swing arm tends to straighten the bike out when slides are attempted and the engine doesn't have enough brute horsepower to override the short arm.

These impressions were made during a one day ride on the R80. We'll have a complete test as soon as a production model is available. But our brief introduction to the bike leads us to believe the R80G/S will be a great machine for exploring the outbacks of Australia or South America or Baja, any place where a combination of dirt roads, secondary paved roads, freeways and you-name-it terrain will be encountered. BMW offers a few accessories to make the outback tourer more comfortable. A saddlebag for the right side of the bike, a rack for the rear fender and a heavy-duty battery for the guy who's planning on adding the electric starter and never wants to use the kick starter. Other accessories are a first aid kit, larger tool kit, case guards, rear mud flap, clock, RPM counter, cylinder protection bars, rubber pads for the foot pegs, shock with reservoir and a lower final drive ratio. Prices for the accessories weren't available yet. The projected price for the R80G/S is $4800.

THE REST OF THE LINE

BMW has trimmed the number of models available in 1981, eliminating the R80 street model. There's still the R65 and four 1000s, the R100RT, R100RS, R100CS and R100. A small-bore version of the 650, the R45 is only available in Europe.

The new models share numerous improvements for 1981. A CD ignition eliminates the BMW's points and condensers. The same steel-silicone coated aluminum cylinders used on the R80 are used, in different sizes, on the 650 and 1000s. The lighter flywheel used on the R80G/S is used on the other models along with the diaphragm-spring clutch pressure plate resulting in 40 percent less lever pressure. Brakes on the entire model line are much

Swing arm has only one arm hence only one shock is used. Final drive is lower than street BMWs. Drive shaft uses the swing arm as a housing. Center stand is stock, side stand is optional. Rear tire can be changed without removing wheel from bike.

Front forks have 7.8 in. of travel. Special tires are made for the BMW by Metzeler. Front brake is a single disc.

Automatic return kickstand has been replaced by a stand that remains down.

improved with the R65-like master cylinder mounted on the handlebars and brake pads designed for better wet-weather braking power.

Forks on the 1000cc BMWs have been given the R65 treatment—damping has been increased for better control. The result is much more positive steering and less brake dive.

The automatic return side stand has

been dropped and a completely new stand that stays put is standard.

On the R100RT are new self-adjusting air shocks at the rear. The pumping action of the shocks raises air pressure to compensate for increasing loads, eliminating the need for a separate air pump.

Add some new paint colors, including a beautiful two-tone gray for the RS and you have it. ◪

BMW R100CS

Big, Simple, Reliable, Light, and Beautiful— The Price Is High But So Is The Quality.

■ Who would call BMW "trend setting?" Even as motorcycles in general have become bigger, faster, more complex with more and more cylinders and valves and carburetors or even computer-controlled  fuel injection, BMWs have come with the same basic engine layout since 1923—opposed Twin, two valves per cylinder, pushrods, two carburetors and a driveshaft to deliver power to the rear wheel.

The 980cc 1981 BMW R100CS is still an opposed Twin, still ohv with pushrods, still shaft-driven, retaining the original concept of the marque even though the design and execution have been refined and honed. It is expensive, selling for $6600, and it is very light, weighing 455 lb. with half a tank of gas.

Simplicity, weight and price are related. BMWs have long been light, some of the low weight coming from simple design and some from the use of lighter, but often more expensive, materials.

The latest trend in Japanese motorcycles is toward lightness. The Kawasaki KZ750 was big news when it was introduced last year, being much lighter than its 750cc competitors at 491 lb. with gas. The Kawasaki KZ1000J, light for a 1000cc Four, weighs 519 lb., and the new Yamaha XV920 V-Twin weighs 519 lb.

BMWs were light before light became fashionable, before that particular trend began in Japanese machines.

Speaking of trends the R100CS is, in a way, one of a line of trend-setters. Elsewhere in this issue there is the Kawasaki 550GPz, which comes with low bars, semi-rearset pegs and a small fairing. Like the Yamaha Seca 550, Suzuki GS450S and Honda CBX, the GPz is the latest sign that the Big Four realize there are people who like sporting bikes.

BMW has known this for years. Back in 1973 there was a policy change and the German factory moved away from its rather stodgy image and got into sports. The result was the R90S. It had—as you've surely guessed—low bars, setback pegs and a bikini fairing.

The R100CS is a direct descendant. BMW has at the same time trimmed and broadened its model line. There's the middleweight R65, the explorer R80GS and four versions of the boxer Twin in 1000cc form; the RT with full fairing and upright

riding position; the RS with a smaller, wind-tunnel-style fairing and lower bars, the standard R100, and the CS, with belly-button fairing.

The BMW's relatively low weight hasn't been used to turn the machine into a high-performance motorcycle. Indeed, the other 1000cc bikes outdistance it in a test of acceleration. The BMW turns the quarter mile in 13.18 sec. with a terminal speed of 101 mph. The XV920 turns 13.06; the KZ1000J, 11.56; the KZ750, 12.26. Even the Seca 550 is quicker, turning 12.99.

The appeal of this BMW, like others of its make, is not rooted in raw horsepower or flashing speed. There is an image of BMWs being reliable and long-lasting. It is, in a sense, self-generating. The image attracts a certain type of rider, a man who values perceived quality above performance, a rider less likely to abuse his bike while hot-rodding around town. BMW buyers are likely to be more mature in age and attitude, and the way they ride contributes to long engine life. Which adds to the image, which attracts more of the same type of rider.

Then, too, BMWs come with relatively tall gearing. The R100CS engine, for example, turns over at a leisurely 3460 rpm at 60 mph in top gear, again contributing to long engine life.

Look at a BMW engine and the most obvious things are the two cylinders, one sticking straight out each side. The placement puts the cylinders and heads and exhaust pipes out into the middle of the airstream, which improves cooling. Each cylinder has a 40mm Bing CV carburetor, the intake manifolds angled inward to give the rider more shin room. Curved rubber tubes lead from the carbs to the airbox, which holds a flat, pleated-paper air filter. Air is drawn into the airbox through two forward-facing plastic snorkels.

The plain-bearing crankshaft runs parallel with the wheelbase, located front-to-back in the frame. The crank throw for the left cylinder is ahead of the crank throw for the right cylinder. Stroke is 70.6mm, while each piston is 94mm in diameter.

New for 1981 are all-aluminum cylinders. Instead of cast-in iron liners, the latest BMW cylinders have a nickle/silicone-carbide coating applied to the bores. BMW engineers say that compared to iron liners, the bore coating increases heat conductivity (and thus, cooling efficiency), reduces break-in time and oil consumption, and makes each cylinder 3 lb. lighter. >

CYCLE WORLD TEST

The camshaft is located in the wet-sump crankcase below the crankshaft, and is driven off the crank by a duplex timing chain. Valves are operated by pushrods via rocker arms, and valve lash is adjusted by conventional screw tappets. The crankcase itself has been made stronger for 1981 and has a larger oil sump.

Also new in this year's BMWs is the clutch assembly, the unit weighing 40 percent less than the 1980 flywheel and clutch. As before, the flywheel is mounted to the crankshaft, with a single automotive-type dry plate carried on a splined transmission input shaft. At the opposite end of the input shaft is a helical gear, which feeds power to the transmission mainshaft. The transmission countershaft is connected directly to the driveshaft coupling, and power is delivered to the driveshaft through two u-joints. The driveshaft runs inside the right swing arm tube and transfers power to the rear wheel through a crown and pinion gearset. The final drive

housing is stronger for 1981, designed for the single-arm, single-shock dual purpose GS but used on dual-arm, dual-shock road models as well.

To meet EPA emissions requirements, air is drawn from the airbox and fed into the exhaust ports through a system of one-way valves and external pipes. Like the system on 1979-and-later Kawasakis, the BMW clean air injection system doesn't use a car-type air pump, but instead relies upon vacuum created in the port by ex-

haust gases rushing out of the cylinder. When the clean air meets the hot exhaust gases, unburned hydrocarbons ignite, reducing emissions.

For the first time on a BMW, an electronic ignition system is used, firing the plugs through new, lighter coils, one coil per cylinder. The exhaust system is changed as well, now using two cross-over tubes (instead of one) between the two separate cylinder exhaust/muffler assemblies.

There was a time when BMWs could be described as being vibration free, at least relative to other machines. But now, when rubber-mounted four-cylinder motorcycle engines are common, the BMW cannot be realistically called smooth throughout the rpm range. Those big, 94mm pistons move back and forth in opposition, that is, each piston starts downward (inward, in this case) from top dead center at the same time. Viewed from the rider's position, when the left piston is traveling to the right, the right piston is traveling to the left. That arrangement tends to cancel out much of the vibration that otherwise would be produced. However, the cylinders fire alternately, so at low rpm (especially below 3000 rpm) vibration from power pulses can be felt through the bars, and images in the mirrors blur. At higher rpm, torsional vibration exists, caused by power being delivered first to the forward throw of the crank, (forcing the front end of the crankshaft to the right), then the rear throw of the crank, (forcing the rear end of the crank to the left). The amount of movement is minute, but it is enough to set up a vibration.

The 1000CS has a classic sweet spot. Between 3000 and 4000 the engine is nice. At 3750 rpm (65 mph) it is perfectly smooth. The mirrors are like, well, like glass. The engine has power and all those little forces cancel each other out, so when it's kept within the rev range it likes, the CS is as smooth and happy as any engine on the market.

The engineers must have known this because the gearing puts this sweet spot right where it does the most good. In top, it's from 50 to 65 mph, while the rider quickly learns to use the gearbox in traffic and when cruising around town.

It is important to note that even below and above that rpm, the kind of vibration produced by the BMW is very different from the high-frequency buzz noticed on higher-revving multis. The BMW's vibration is well controlled and of low frequency, and it is not intrusive or annoying even on long trips. Just how different vibration can be is best illustrated by jumping off a Suzuki GS850 and climbing onto an R100CS. Both are absolutely, perfectly smooth compared to a Harley-Davidson Sportster or a Triumph Bonneville. But in actual fact, the Suzuki has an underlying buzz felt through the bars, and the BMW has an underlying succession of pulses, a muted sort of low-frequency vibration, reminders that very large pistons are moving under the force of alternating explosions of vaporized gasoline. Running at higher speeds for long distances gives the impression of the engine working, and the faster it runs, the more vivid the perceived pulses through the bars.

This year's engine gains revs much more rapidly than last year's, due to the lighter flywheel and shifts better, too. The clunk that used to accompany each shift is gone, and because the engine can change speed quickly with the reduction in flywheel weight, the tendency to miss shifts or have difficulty shifting is gone. That's good, because in the case of a missed shift bringing rpm much over the 7200 rpm redline, it is common for those great big pistons to collide with the equally-big exhaust valves, requiring a top-end overhaul before its time. This BMW may not buzz like a Suzuki, but then it can't be revved to 10,500 rpm either.

While the R100CS accelerates and shifts better than previous BMWs, it still gets good gas mileage, 50 mpg on the *Cycle World* mileage test loop, and because it comes with a large gas tank, it has exceptional traveling range, about 265 mi. before reserve.

In keeping with BMW's penchant for simplicity, the R100CS has standard forks without air adjustability, without preload adjustability, without damping adjustability. The rear shocks have adjustable preload, period. Which means that the selection of damping and preload and spring rates must be a compromise suited to a wide range of uses and rider weights, and that compromise shows up when a 140-lb. rider encounters successive small bumps, like concrete highway expansion joints. Then the BMW's suspension is not as compliant as the suspension on a GS1100 set on the softest settings, and the jolts reach the rider and make the speedometer and tachometer bobble up and down on their rubber mounts. The bike does handle well at high speed on smoother surfaces.

In street corners, the footpegs on each side drag first, and it will take a brave soul to drag the cylinder heads. On the racetrack, it is possible to drag the heads on each side, with the stock Metzeler street tires.

Because it is light and because the center of gravity is relatively low, the BMW responds more quickly and easily to rider input in ess turns, making an accurate transition from right to left to right without hesitation. But the rider must be careful of two things if the bike is ridden at top speed. First, upon accelerating over abrupt, drastic pavement changes or potholes at speed, the front end feels very light, as if the front wheel isn't staying on the ground, and the bike changes direction and the handlebars wiggle back and forth as the front wheel is deflected. To its credit, the bike will return to its original course without requiring any action by the rider other than hanging on.

Next, BMW engineers may have preceeded the Japanese craze for low weight and even the current trend of shaft drive, but they still haven't figured out how to eliminate driveshaft-induced torque reactions in the rear end of a motorcycle. The lighter flywheel seems to accentuate and >

draw attention to the unchanged driveshaft reaction. Grab a handful of throttle and the rear shocks extend, the rear of the seat rising as the driveshaft pinion works against the ring gear in the final drive. Slam the throttle shut, and the rear end sags. Even when the rider is careful and the throttle is not worked rapidly to the extremes, the rise and fall of the rear end is pronounced and very real. Holding the gas on over a dip in the road will prevent the shocks from absorbing that dip, an advantage perhaps if the dip would normally cause the shocks to bottom, a disadvantage if the dip is at a corner exit and inaction of the shocks causes the rear tire to slide under power.

Enter a turn leaned over to the limits and close the throttle, and the ground clearance will be reduced. To be ridden at the limits the BMW demands adjustments in approach. Several other motor-

cycles with driveshafts, including the Suzuki GS650, the Yamaha Seca 750 and the Honda CX500, have less torque reaction at the rear wheel.

This year all the BMWs larger than the R65 get new forks, leading axle style with the usual long travel, but with better damping control than that of previous BMW forks. Instead of the rocking horse motion that used to come when a BMW's brakes were applied, the new forks behave much more predictably because of the improved damping. Ride quality of the forks is at least as good as the old models, perhaps better.

Evaluating the ride quality of a BMW means coming to grips with the seat. It's a reasonably sized and shaped seat, with very firm padding and a tendency to break-in or develop a new shape as it's sat on for long periods of time. Because the seat is much firmer than many of the other

big bikes, it makes small bumps more noticeable and that makes the suspension seem to be harsher than it really is. In any case, the BMW doesn't have one of those seats that everyone immediately liked, but it is possible to survive on it for quite some distance.

Interesting, too, is the failure of BMW engineers to come to grips with sidestand and centerstand placement and design. True, the centerstand's position is such that if the rear wheel is removed, the bike rocks forward, perched on stand and front wheel. If the front wheel is removed, the bike rocks back, supported by stand and rear wheel. But it is also true that reaching and using the centerstand is difficult; that once the centerstand is lowered by a small extension on its left side, then the rider must shift his foot inward onto the main part of the stand to deploy it, and that during the foot shift the stand has an an-

New final drive hub unit is stronger, designed for use on R80/GS but used on road models (like R100CS) as well.

R100CS main frame backbone contains a retractable, locking cable to secure the bike.

R100CS instruments include the usual speedometer and tachometer, as well as a voltmeter and a clock. Choke lever is on left handlebar control pod.

Handlebar-mount sport fairing keeps wind off the rider's chest, but directs it at the helmet.

BMW R100CS

SPECIFICATIONS

List price $6600
Engine ......ohv opposed Twin
Bore x stroke ....94 x 70.6mm
Displacement...........980cc
Compression ratio.......8.2:1
Carburetion........ (2) 40mm
Bing CV
Air filter ....pleated paper
Ignition...........transistorized
electronic
Claimed power ....na
Claimed torque ....na
Lubrication ....wet sump
Oil capacity ....2.6 qt.
Fuel capacity ....6.3 gal.
Starter ....electric
Electrical power.........280w
alternator
Battery 12v 28ah
Headlight 60/55w
Primary drive .....helical gear
Clutch ....single plate, dry
Final drive ....drive shaft

Gear ratios, overall:1
5th 4.4
4th 4.9
3rd 6.0
2nd 8.3
1st 12.8

Suspension:
Front ....telescopic fork
travel ....8.0 in.
Rear.............swing arm
travel ....4.9 in.

Tires:
Front..............3.25H-19
Metzeler ME11
Rear..............4.00H-18
Metzeler ME77

Brakes:
Front........(2) 10.125 in.
hydraulic discs
Rear............7.8-in. drum
Brake swept area 187.3 sq. in.
Brake loading (160-lb.
rider) ....3.28 lb./sq. in.
Wheelbase ....58 in.
Rake/Trail ....28°/3.7 in.
Handlebar width ....24 in.
Seat height ....31 in.
Seat width ....10 in.
Footpeg height ....11 in.
Ground clearance ....5.5 in.
Test weight
(w/half-tank fuel) ..455 lb.
Weight bias,
front/rear % 45/55
GVWR ....876 lb.
Load capacity ....421 lb.

ACCELERATION

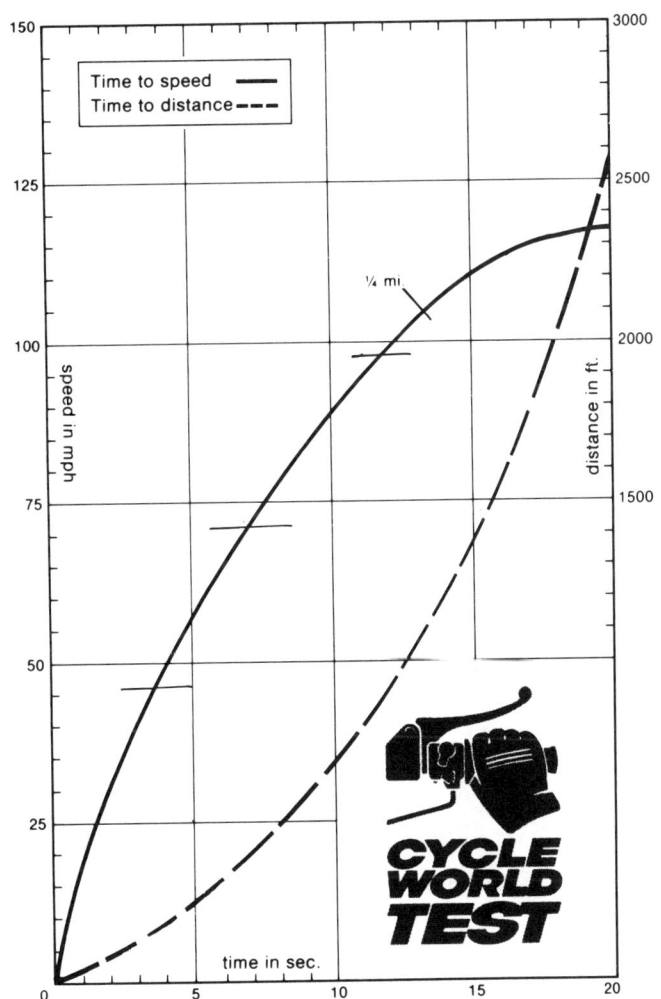

Time to speed ——
Time to distance – – –

¼ mi.

speed in mph

distance in ft.

time in sec.

CYCLE WORLD TEST

PERFORMANCE

Standing ¼-mile....13.18 sec.
@ 101.12 mph

Top speed in ½-mile .114 mph

Fuel consumption......50 mpg

Range
(to reserve tank) ...265 mi.

Acceleration:
0–30 mph .... 2.0 sec.
0–40 mph .... 2.9 sec.
0–50 mph .... 4.0 sec.
0–60 mph .... 5.3 sec.
0–70 mph .... 7.1 sec.
0–80 mph .... 8.7 sec.
0–90 mph .... 10.3 sec.
0–100 mph .... 12.9 sec.

Top gear acceleration:
40–60 mph .... 4.4 sec.
60–80 mph ....5.8 sec.

Maximum speed in gears:
1st.................. 44 mph
2nd.................. 68 mph
3rd.................. 94 mph
4th.................. 115 mph
5th.................128 mph

Speedometer error:
30 mph indicated 29.67 mph
60 mph indicated 60.28 mph

Braking distance:
from 30 mph.......... 32 ft.
from 60 mph........ 132 ft.

Engine speed
at 60 mph........ 3460rpm

noying tendency to spring upward into the retracted position; that the centerstand itself is too narrow to support the bike securely on uneven, rough, or sloped pavement; that reaching and deploying the sidestand is almost impossible to do without first getting off the bike and groping with the toe. There must be, and are, better ways to build stands.

Footpeg position, happily, has been improved. But the higher, more forward pegs are still so close to the passenger pegs that a passenger's feet hit the rider's feet if the passenger pegs are adjusted to the forward position. And BMW issued a recall earlier this year of right-hand footpegs, saying that the peg location was dangerous and prevented easy reach of the rear brake lever. Our test bike was delivered before the recall, and it was difficult to reach the rear brake quickly.

The rear brake is a mechanically-operated drum, the front a double-disc activated by hydraulic pressure with Brembo calipers. The front master cylinder is located on the right handlebar. The 10.125-in. discs are small compared to many other machines, but yield good braking power for the weight and speed of the bike. Brake feel was a matter of controversy among staff members, some thinking the front brake felt mushy, some thinking it was fine. The brakes on 1981 BMWs are better than those on previous models.

Horns. Happily, the horns on the BMW are state-of-the-art, making one wonder why all bikes don't have such wonderful, loud, effective horns. Same for the big quartz-halogen headlight. Instruments are well-lit and easy to read, including the fairing-mounted clock and voltmeter, and accurate.

BMW controls are different and interesting. After years of staying with the up-down turn signal switch while everybody except Harley-Davidson used right-left, BMW has gone to right-left for the signals. At the same time the horn button is at the top of the cluster, a distance from the rider's thumb, and the signal switch is at the bottom, opposite to what the others have. No big deal; BMW buyers tend to keep their bikes for years and don't swap brands much, but for the first few days it *is* likely you'll intend to politely signal and will instead rudely honk, or vice versa.

Latest version of BMW's ohv flat Twin has all-alloy cylinder, air injection into exhaust ports to control emissions, and new airbox/air filter assembly.

The plastic tray seen over the battery holds the exceptional tool kit. Bing carbs are changed for 1981. One bolt secures rocker cover.

More important in the long run is the sad fact that BMW no longer fits a standard throttle stop. There's no way to set the throttle for cruising and the return springs are much firmer than two CV carbs warrant.

The finish of everything—castings, paint, stampings . . . everything—makes the typical mass-produced motorcycle look, upon close examination, cheap, unfinished. Examine the fins on a BMW cylinder or the finish of the cases, and you'll not find any defects hidden by thick paint. The welds are works of art, the pin stripes hand-painted instead of being stuck-on decals, the fenders light-but-pricy fiberglass instead of cheap and heavy stamped steel.

The tool kit is a real, usable set of tools, not pot-metal imitations of tools, that fit and can be used to do major work on the motorcycle. Included are tire irons capable of removing a tire, a patch kit capable of patching an inner tube, and a tire pump capable of inflating a tire.

Maintenance is simple and straightforward—one bolt secures each rocker cover, and valve adjustment is via screw tappets. There are, of course, only four valves total to adjust on the motorcycle.

The rear hub is cleverly designed so that the ring gear and brake assembly stay in place when the rear wheel is removed, the wheel hub including a spline that fits into the drive assembly. To remove the rear wheel, one pinch bolt must be loosened on the left end of the axle, and one axle nut (on the right side of the axle) removed. Then the axle easily slides clear and the rear wheel comes out while the bike is supported by the center stand and front wheel. It takes about two minutes.

It's possible to buy a BMW, ride off the showroom floor, with nothing except riding gear and the bike, travel out onto the highway, get a flat tire, repair the flat tire, and continue on your way, no truck needed.

That's something, right there. In fact, we can't name a single other brand of motorcycle that comes, standard, with the same degree of self-sufficiency and ability to be maintained and repaired by the owner.

We can't think of another brand of bike which is finished as nicely, either.

Which, we're sure, has a lot to do with why the BMW—1923 concept through 1981 execution—is alive and well in America today. ◘

BMW R100RS/E
Something New in Current Technology

CYCLE WORLD TEXT

■ Entirely new motorcycles from BMW aren't announced every year, or every decade for that matter. This doesn't mean that the famous German marque hasn't been actively working to improve its product. While producing the traditional opposed Twin for the past 50-some years, BMW engineers have been working on alternate engine configurations and alternate power sources even. Rumors in the European magazines have been predicting the imminent arrival of the new BMW, which, according to usually unreliable sources, was to be an inline Four, or a Triple or a V-Four. It was also rumored to be either air or liquid cooled and to have a driveshaft. Engine size was anticipated to be around one liter.

Prototype BMWs have been seen using various engines, or so it seemed. Because of the importance of the U.S. motorcycle market to BMW, the bike is being tested in this country. During testing of the secret motorcycle at Laguna Seca raceway in California, *CW* contributor Ron Hussey spied the motorcycle and took several photos before BMW noticed him standing on the track with a 500mm lens and offered to let us test the bike.

This is a prototype, with many parts that will be changed before the bike goes into production. Also, certain details of the machine's internals aren't available. As the photos show, this new machine looks much like the existing R100RS. The RS fairing and even some engine parts have been attached to the experimental model to hide the new powerplant. Secrecy has been important to BMW because of the radical nature of the new machine.

So far none of the rumors has come close to identifying the shocking difference in the new machine.

It's electric! Yes, BMW has perfected the electric motorcycle. This was not the original design BMW intended, but after years of working with coal-gas powered external combustion engines and even micro-nuclear powered machines, the company has settled on electric power. It was in the Twenties that the company engineers started working on the steam cycle. Current technology led them to try electricity.

The electric cycle has a number of inherent advantages, which our brief test

R100RS/E

ride of the prototype machine demonstrates. And it offers considerable development potential. The threat of various government regulations mean nothing to the electric cycle. There are no exhaust emissions, so of course there is no sacrifice in power or rideability to meet present or future standards. And proposed noise standards won't be a bother either. Even at full acceleration the bike only makes a muffled "ooooohm" sound that's no louder than a vacuum cleaner. The electric motorcycle is also immune to the whims of Arab oil-mongers. Just pull into your neighborhood service station and say, "Charge it."

An electric motor makes for a simple machine, in the BMW tradition. There are no carburetors or points or air filter or oil, so maintenance is reduced to nothing. Even long-term maintenance shouldn't amount to more than new brushes, bushings and a Bendix drive. This simple device doesn't need a transmission or clutch because the engine develops full torque at low engine speeds and when the machine comes to a stop the motor just stops, too. It doesn't need to idle. A digital-analog rheostate controls engine speed, which then controls the bike's speed.

Performance is more than adequate, in the usual BMW style. High gearing and the choice of batteries has produced a machine with high top speed and acceleration that is only a little slower than the best the competition has to offer. Measured at the half mile by our calibrated radar gun, the electric BMW has a top speed of 134.4 fpcf (furlongs per centi-fortnight.) Acceleration through the quarter-furlong took

22.5 sec., but familiarity with the controls and a larger rear tire would probably bring that figure down about six or seven seconds.

Contributing to the slightly slow quarter-furlong time was a rather high weight of 541 g. This is surprising because BMW has been a leader in producing lightweight motorcycles. Company engineers say that when the camouflage covers are removed on the production models the weight will be substantially reduced.

Many of the bike's good points are apparent only out on the highway. The machine is, literally, as smooth as an electric motor. There are fewer controls on this machine and the entire motorcycle falls readily to hand. While the seat is harder than usual for a BMW, it is admirably low and our smaller test riders enjoyed being able to put their feet flat on the ground at stoplights. Larger riders were a bit cramped on the machine.

Running characteristics are wonderful. There is no hesitation or stumble during acceleration. It also doesn't matter to the motorcycle whether it is 20° or 100° because it doesn't have to atomize any gasoline. Handling is quick and sure. The wheelbase is somewhat shorter than a normal BMW, which makes steering faster. Changes in direction can be made almost instantly without hanging off or perceptable movement of the handlebars. On rough surfaces the bike is a bit unstable and one of our test riders fell off several times trying to run over a small bump, but the machine and rider survived intact, ready to try it again. Brakes are more than adequate for the speed and weight of the machine, are easily controllable but make the rider's hair stand on end when applied in the rain. A little work here is in order.

Overall, we are impressed with this new BMW. Not all riders were equally excited by it, but there were generally more positive than negative comments about the electric BMW. One person said the styling was re–volting, but he's an old fuddy-duddy anyway. Most people thought it was pleasantly flashy. Certainly this is going to shock the Japanese motorcycle producers who may be surprised by the under-$100 price expected for the production model. At that price BMW will have overcome the major problem facing the company in this country for years and it should find little resistance in the marketplace. ◙

BMW R100RS/E

SPECIFICATIONS

List price................$29.95
Engine ....:.......electric
Bore x
    stroke .....none to speak of
Displacement ....16 oz.
Compression ratio 1:1
Carburetion ....no
Air filter ....in helmet
Ignition......................liftoff
Claimed power ..54.7 Newton
    meters/sec.^{2}@1750 rpm
Claimed torque ..67.5 oz.-ft. @
    1 rpm
Lubrication system ....perman-
    ently lubricated bushings
Oil Capacity ....0.02 cc
Fuel capacity ......3 batteries
Starter ....button
Electrical power ......3v + 9v
Battery ....(2) AA
Headlight ....brilliant
Primary drive ....shaft
Clutch ....two hands
    5th 1
    4th 1
    3rd 1
    2nd 1
    1st 1
Suspension:
    Front ....telescopic fork
        travel ....6.9 mm
    Rear..............swing arm
        travel ....4.1 mm
Tires:
    Front.....3.25-18 Continent
    Rear..........4.25-18 Island
Brakes:
    Front.............. dual disc
    Rear.................... disc
Brake swept area ..39 sq. mm
Brake loading (160-lb.
    rider) .....4.14 lb./sq. mm
Wheelbase ....6.1 in.
Rake/Trail ......28°/4.56 mm
Handlebar width.........2.6 in.
Seat height ....3.4 in.
Seat width ....1.3 in.
Test weight
    (w/half-tank fuel) ...541 g.
Weight bias,
    % front/rear, ...54/46
GVWR ....998 g.
Load capacity ....457 g.

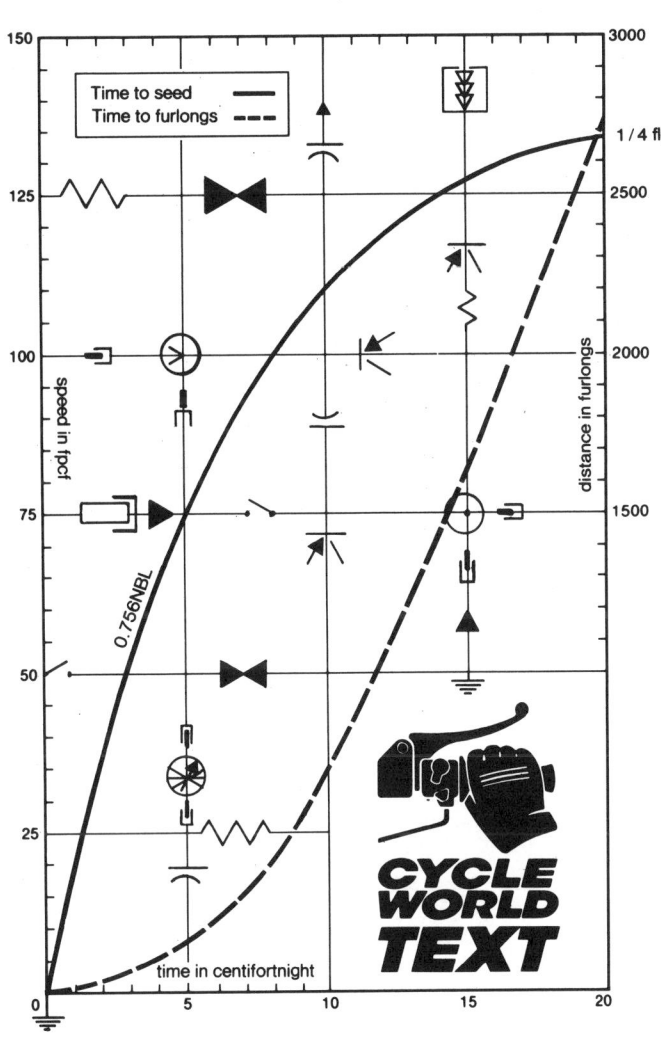

0.756NBL

speed in fpcf

distance in furlongs

time in centifortnight

Time to seed ——
Time to furlongs - - -

1/4 flg

CYCLE WORLD TEXT

PERFORMANCE

Standing ¼-flg ...22.5 sec. @
    134 fpcf
Top speed in ½-flg ....134 fpcf
Fuel consumption ...14 ma/flg
Range
    (to reserve tank) ..... home
                                on the,
Acceleration:
    0–30 fpcf......... 1.8 blinks
    0–40 fpcf......... 2.8 blinks
    0–50 fpcf......... 3.1 blinks
    0–60 fpcf......... 4.5 blinks
    0–70 fpcf......... 5.7 blinks
    0–80 fpcf......... 7.8 blinks
    0–90 fpcf.......10.2 blinks
    0–100 fpcf ......14.7 blinks
Top gear acceleration:
    40–60 fpcf...............4.5
    60–80 fpcf 5.3
Maximum speed in gears:
    1st................. 134 fpcf
    2nd................. 134 fpcf
    3rd................. 134 fpcf
    4th................. 134 fpcf
    5th ....134 fpcf
Speedometer error:
    30 mph indicated.........40
    60 mph indicated 40
Braking distance:
    from 30 ....28 in.
    from 60 ....134 in.
Engine speed
    at 60 ....857 rpm

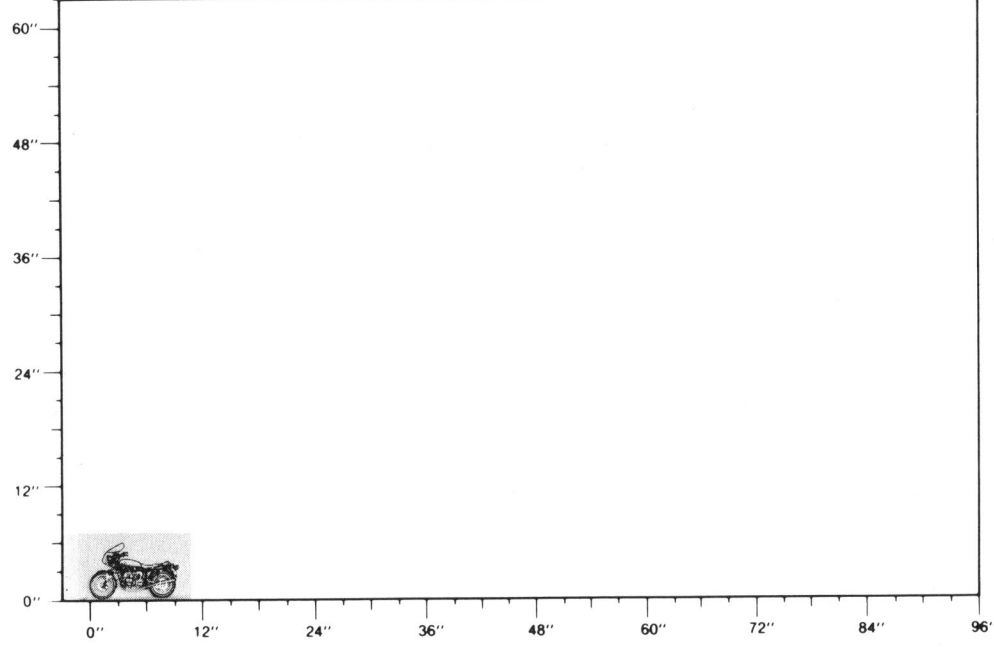

■ As we left the diner a man came over and asked if the BMW R65LS was turbocharged. No, we told him. Oh, he said, walking away. Later at the gas station the attendant took our card and asked if the bike had "any computer stuff" on it. No, we said, and he looked disappointed. Riding home that night the R75 rider pu'led up at a stoplight and yelled across, 'Is that a thousand?" "It's a 650," we yelled back. He disappeared before the next stoplight.

That's the kind of bike BMW's sporting new R65LS is. It looks exciting, it looks fast, it looks modern and if it's exciting and fast and modern it must be computerized, turbocharged and have at least 1000cc.

Despite the Gee Whiz styling, the R65LS is the kind of bike BMW has specialized in for years: light, simple, agile and well finished. The engine is the 650cc ohv opposed Twin shared with the standard R65. Bore is 82mm, stroke is 61.5mm, compression ratio is 8.2:1, carburetors are 32mm Bing CV. This is not the same engine used on the larger BMWs, being a short-stroke version. It was introduced with the R65 and European-only R45 in 1979. The standard BMW engine has a 70.6mm stroke, whether it is used in a 600cc bike or the 1000cc bikes currently in production. Shortening the stroke for the R65 makes the engine narrower than it would be if the longer stroke were used, and it also enables the engine to have a relatively larger bore and thus bigger valves.

Valve sizes on the R65 are 40mm for the intake and 36mm for the exhaust, each held open for 308° as are all BMW valves. Being extremely oversquare, the BMW's piston speeds are quite low for its size. That's because the R65 stroke is about the same as a Honda 750 Four that revs much higher. This low piston speed is not used to tune the machine for great peak power at high revs, but instead is used to keep rings and cylinders from wearing out quickly. Maximum engine speed of the R65 is listed at 7650 rpm, while maximum continuous speed (a peculiarly German distinction) is 7300 rpm. These are not high engine speeds. The BMW's cam is not timed for great engine speed.

Compression ratio on the latest BMWs of all sizes has been lowered from 9.2:1 to 8.2. This has been done so BMWs can run on low octane fuel without detonation, and the test R65 had no trouble on regular, unleaded or high octane fuels.

Other changes have been made in the last two years to bring BMWs into the Eighties. Ignition is now triggered electronically, which is particularly appreci- →

BMW R65LS
What's a Paint Job Like This Doing on a BMW?

R65LS

ated on the BMW because setting the points on a BMW used to be more of a bother than it should have been. Fortunately ignition timing is still adjustable, unlike some other bikes with electronic systems. That can be appreciated if a particular machine is prone to detonation or can run with increased advance at high elevations.

To meet emission rules BMW has added an air breather to the exhaust ports, much like the system used by Kawasaki. This helps oxidize the emissions in the exhaust so the carbs don't have to be leaned out excessively. At least in theory they don't have to be leaned out too much. The parts to adapt the exhaust breather to the BMW are simple enough, some one-way valves and steel tubes connecting the exhaust ports with the new airbox. Older BMWs used a cast aluminum chamber above the transmission to house the air filter. Now there's an easily removable flat paper filter housed in a plastic chamber installed where the old casting used to be. The new airbox also includes breather tubes routing blowby from the crankcase to the intake tubes between the airbox and the carburetors.

Last year's major changes to the engine were the addition of all-alloy cylinders and a new clutch. The cylinders are a high silicon alloy with a nickel bore surface. According to BMW the new cylinders, used on all the BMW models, are three times better for heat transfer than the steel-lined cylinders, plus needing less break-in and having reduced oil consumption. All that and the new cylinders are 6. lb. lighter than the steel-lined cylinders.

Like the new cylinders, the clutch change was introduced last year on all the BMWs. The new clutch is 8 lb. lighter than the clutch used on the big BMWs, plus it uses a diaphragm spring pressure plate for more positive action and lighter clutch pull. It is still a single plate dry clutch.

What hasn't been changed is the chassis. When the R65 was introduced it had the first new BMW frame and suspension in years. The double downtube cradle frame used smaller round tubing for the main section and had a different bolt-on rear section than the big BMW frame. The forks were an entirely new straight-leg design with substantially different suspension qualities than the leading-axle forks on the bigger BMWs. Travel was only 6.8 in. instead of 8.2 in. as used previously. And the fork spring on the 650 BMW is a single rate moderate tension spring instead of the double rate too-soft primary and firm secondary. When the R65 was introduced it was the best handling stock BMW, being easier to control than the large BMWs because the sus-

pension didn't allow the bike to discover as many unusual attitudes as the older long-travel suspension.

Apparently the new style suspension has satisfied BMW because the new large BMWs now have forks that work more like the R65 forks. And the new larger BMWs have also moved the front brake master cylinder from under the gas tank to the handlebars, where it doesn't need to be cable-actuated. Enhancing the braking ability of the LS is the addition of a second disc brake on the front wheel. Both discs are 10.25 in. across, drilled for lightness, and grabbed by Brembo calipers. Combined with the 1mm smaller master cylinder bore used on the LS, the braking power of the machine is excellent.

An 8.7 in. drum is used for a rear brake on the LS, a particularly good choice. It is strong enough for the job, easily controlled, works in the rain and, in conjunction with the driveshaft assembly on the righthand side of the swing arm, it enables the rear wheel to be pulled with less time and effort than any other street bike.

At both ends of the LS are wheels quite unlike anything that's ever appeared on a motorcycle before. First, they are antiseptic white. People who see the wheels are inclined to touch them to see if they are plastic, they are so clean and light-looking. Construction of the wheels is accordingly unusual. Rims are hardened aluminum. The spokes are cast of a softer alloy so the wheels have some flex while possessing adequate rim strength. In shape the wheel spokes are built out of two shapes, five elongated ovals in the center of the wheel tied to five triangular shapes of spoke extending to the rim. The white surface is hard enough to resist scratching and chipping in normal use and is smooth enough so it can be cleaned more easily than normal cast wheels. Rim diameter is 18 in. at both ends, 1.85 in. wide in front and 2.50 in. wide in back. Tubes are used in the Continental tires.

As nice as the mechanical components of the motorcycle are, it is the appearance that makes this bike. And nothing contributes more to the stunning appearance of the LS than the brilliant red paint. This is not fire engine red, or Italian motorcycle red. It's brighter than any other red, with just a touch of orange to the color. On the BMW it is also perfectly applied to the pleasantly large 5.8 gal. gas tank, the molded plastic front fender, the plastic tailpiece and the plastic cow catcher around the headlight. Most of these components would probably be embarassed to be called plastic. They don't look plastic any more than the wheels look like aluminum. Take the front fender, for instance. It's stiff and feels like a well-made stamped steel fender. Only the edges aren't rolled under. Thinking the fender was cast metal, we examined it with a magnet to see if it was steel. It

wasn't. The piece is nothing like the plastic fenders found on other bikes. It is solid enough it could work as a fork brace. And the finish is perfect.

If the cow catcher looks related to something on a Suzuki Katana, you have an astute eye. The design concept comes from the same man. Only the BMW is much more subdued, as a BMW should be. BMW claims the mini-fairing reduces front end lift by a third while improving riding comfort. The black plastic shield that continues above the headlight, then folds down to enclose the instruments and continues on down around the handlebars might just do something to break up some wind to hit the rider. Then again, it might not. Any difference is so slight riders weren't aware of any protection. What is obvious is that no other fairing or windshield will fit on the LS with the cow catcher in place. Removing the nose isn't easy either, as it forms the instrument housing. It would take a callous person to make that change to the bike's appear-

ance. Sort of like giving Meryl Streep a nose job so she could wear glasses more easily.

Another piece on the LS that establishes its appearance is the seat. It's black and covered in the usual naugaskin, but it doesn't have a pattern that looks like your wife accidentally left a hot waffle iron on the seat. There is no stitching or embossed pattern, and there's no grab strap running across the seat right where you want to sit. This is probably the cleanest design on a seat ever. It's padded a little better than some other BMW seats, though it's not pillow-soft. And the passenger can use grab handles built into the tailpiece if they are necessary.

Lifting the hinged tailpiece is easy enough after pushing a button. It can be locked, but that's not mandatory. Under the seat is a larger storage bin at the back of the motorcycle and a large bin behind the gas tank for tools. BMW is one of the very few motorcycle companies that doesn't put a few imitation tools into a >

BMW R65LS

SPECIFICATIONS

List price $3995
Engine ......ohv opposed Twin
Bore x stroke....82 x 61.5mm
Displacement............650cc
Compression ratio.......8.2:1
Carburetion........ (2) 32mm
Bing CV
Air filter ....dry paper
Ignition ....electronic
Claimed power ....na
Claimed torque ....na
Lubrication ....wet sump
Oil capacity ....2.6 qt.
Fuel capacity ....5.8 gal.
Starter ....electric
Electrical power..........280w
alternator
Battery ....12v / 16ah
Headlight ....55/60w halogen
Primary drive ....direct
Clutch ....dry single plate
Final drive ....shaft
Gear ratios, overall:1
5th 5.17
4th 5.75
3rd 7.13
2nd 9.85
1st 15.16
Suspension:
Front ....telescopic fork
travel ....6.9 in.
Rear............. swing axle
travel ....4.3 in.
Tires:
Front..............3.25H-18
Continental RB2
Rear.............. 4.00 H-18
Continental K112A
Brakes:
Front.....dual 10.25-in. disc
Rear............8.7 in. drum
Brake swept area ..255 sq. in.
Brake loading (160lb.
rider) ....2.34 lb. / sq. in.
Wheelbase ....55.4 in.
Rake/Trail ....28°/3.8 in.
Handlebar width ....24.5 in.
Seat height ....31.3 in.
Seat width ....8 in.
Footpeg height ....12 in.
Ground clearance ......5.4 in.
Test weight
(w/half-tank fuel) ..438 lb.
Weight bias,
% front/rear..........45/55
GVWR ....878 lb.
Load capacity ....440 lb.

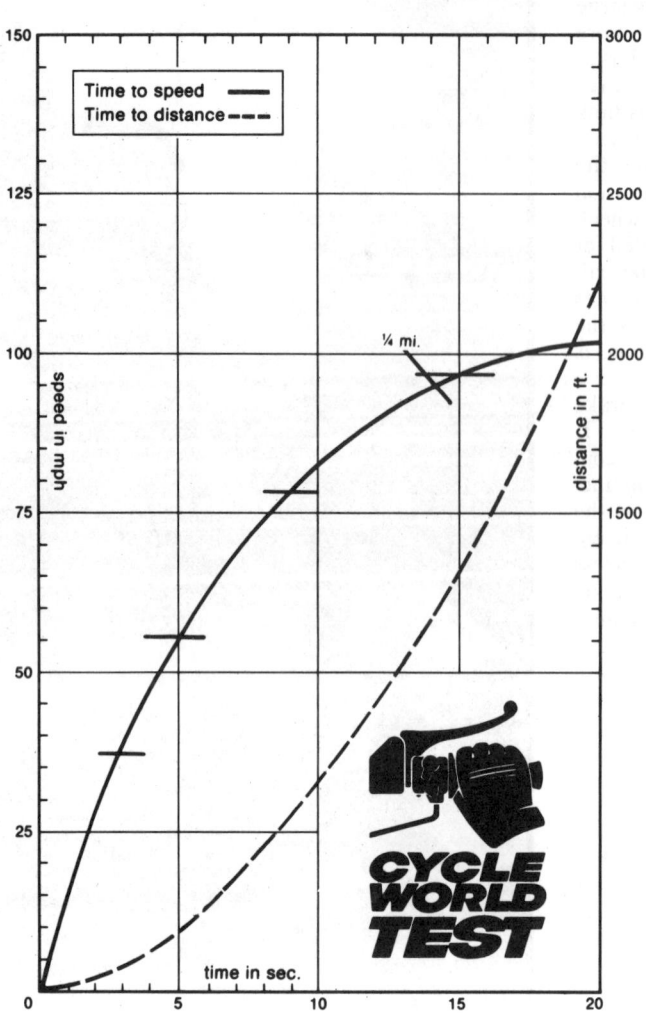

Time to speed ——
Time to distance ---

150 — 3000
speed in mph
distance in ft.
¼ mi.
125 — 2500
100 — 2000
75 — 1500
50
25
time in sec.
0 5 10 15 20

CYCLE WORLD TEST

PERFORMANCE

Standing ¼-mile....13.99 sec.
@ 93.16 mph
Top speed in
½-mile ....101 mph
Fuel consumption......53 mpg
Range
(to reserve tank) ...265 mi.
Acceleration:
0–30 mph......... 2.2 sec.
0–40 mph......... 3.1 sec.
0–50 mph......... 4.1 sec.
0–60 mph......... 5.5 sec.
0–70 mph......... 7.7 sec.
0–80 mph.......10.5 sec.
0–90 mph.........13.2 sec.
Top gear acceleration:
40–60 mph........ 6.4 sec.
60–80 mph ....10.9 sec.
Maximum speed in gears:
1st..................38 mph
2nd..................58 mph
3rd..................80 mph
4th..................99 mph
5th.................110 mph
Speedometer error:
30 mph indicated... 30 mph
60 mph indicated ..59 mph
Braking distance:
from 30 mph..........39 ft.
from 60 mph ....139 ft.
Engine speed
at 60 mph 4088

R65LS

plastic bag exactly big enough for all the tools except for the pliers.

No longer does BMW include tire patching equipment in the tool kit, but all these nice BMW tools are still there except for the air pump, tire irons and patch kit. And those parts are optional. Even the tire pump mounting lugs are still on the bike. During testing the rear tire picked up a nail and we had the opportunity (?) to notice some nice attention to details when changing it. The rear tire can be removed in about a minute by removing one nut and loosening one bolt. As the tire slips off the splines the machine pivots forward, resting on the front tire. Even changing the tire in our own shop we used the BMW's tool kit because it was just as convenient as using our own tools. Because the tires have tubes, it is easier to break the bead on the BMW tires than on most of the tubeless designs. There is an inner lip on the rims to keep the tire in place when flat, a good safety feature, but it doesn't interfere much in tire changing. The smooth white surface makes easy work of running the tire on and off the rim, but the edges get chipped easily with any normal tire irons.

Most basic maintenance on the BMW is so easy as to be inviting. Rocker arm covers come off with one bolt. Valve lash is easily adjusted with simple tools and there are only four valves to adjust. Even changing the air filter doesn't require any tools.

Accentuating the ease of service is the wonderful owner's manual. Most motorcycle owner's manuals have become nothing more than defenses in product liability suits, filled with lots of warnings and cautions and notes, but no information about how to maintain a motorcycle. Not this one. The explanations are clear and understandable. Photos are well done. The warnings in this manual are reasonable and worth reading. There are even recommendations on extra parts that might be needed on an extended journey. Service procedures are explained for checking and changing all fluid levels, for changing brake pads, checking wheel bearings, removing wheels, changing tires, replacing light bulbs, adjusting valves, checking the timing, adjusting carburetors and numerous other routine chores. Even torque figures are included for most major bolts and tightening sequences are listed for head bolts. These may not be things all owners will want to tackle, but it is information that BMW trusts its owners with and we only wish more motorcycle companies would do so.

As modern and well thought out as the R65LS is, it is not a motorcycle that can be ridden without adaptation by the rider. All BMWs have quirks that riders of other brands usually find disconcerting at first. Some of the quirks turn out to be appreciated features later on, and some of them remain nuisances.

Most unusual of the bike's characteristics is the seating position. It is sporting in a way that Japanese bikes even with red paint have not discovered. The handlebars are low and narrow, with little rise. The pegs do not fold and are thus placed relatively high, though they may be adjusted on their mounts. One does not sit bolt upright on this bike without having spent prior time on the rack. There are no arms that long.

So the LS rider leans forward. This works well when the bike is on the road, in top gear, going at speeds where the winds of motion help support the rider. For that kind of riding the position is correct. At lower speeds a rider must hold himself up in a semi-pushup position. That can be tiring. The riding position combines with the short bars and the bike's quick steering to surprise first-time riders. These are not bars that can be pulled to steer the bike. Instead, the rider's weight is resting on the handlebars and normal pushing and pulling doesn't produce the same amount of turn as on most other bikes this size.

This is only a factor for about a week of riding. After that a rider learns how the BMW likes to be steered, using forward motion on the bars to get surprisingly quick results. The LS is a quick steering bike and it is responsive, even though the efforts to produce that steering are somewhat higher than normal.

Suspension control helps the LS. This is not a foamy-feeling suspension. Spring and damping rates are well matched. The result is a taut suspension with plenty of travel for large bumps and dips but less compliance for small irregularities than many of the softer sprung Japanese bikes. That slightly stiffer suspension also enables the LS to handle the weight of a passenger.

How comfortable the bike is depends on the conditions. For freeway use the bike is not as plush as a GL500. But it is not a tiring bike to ride, being much lighter than a Silver Wing and more fun to fling around crooked roads. Vibration is noticeable, more so at around 4000 rpm than other speeds. It isn't a great amount of vibration and, being a Twin, the frequency is low. It is also much smoother than conventional parallel Twins without counterbalancer shafts.

Controls are not all placed in the most convenient locations. Brake and clutch levers are fine and the efforts needed for operation are pleasantly low. The throttle return springs may be a trifle stiff. Worse is the position of the lefthand switches. In order to place the rearview mirror where it is in any way useful, the turn signal switch is much too low for easy reach. The horn is at the top of the control pod and is easily reached and the high beam switch, with its easy-to-use high beam flasher, is convenient enough. Perhaps on a bike with more normal handlebars the switch wouldn't have to be twisted down so far for the mirrors to be used.

Other controls are fine. The ignition switch is right between the instruments where it's easy to reach. Even a choke lever is installed at the left hand grip where it can be manipulated while the bike tries to start. This is a good thing, too, because the bike does not like running when it is cold.

Normal procedure is to give full choke and hit the starter button. The engine usually fires right up and then dies just as quickly. Giving a little gas helps. About six firings are needed to get the bike out of the driveway. This could stand some improvement.

When warm the engine fires right up and runs well. Well, it runs okay. Most of the time. There is, however, quite a lean spot at 4000 to 5000 rpm. Cruising at this speed, and it is a very common cruising speed, causes the bike to run as though it were running out of gas. Above 5000 rpm the engine runs especially well, revving freely and powerfully. Low rpm power is adequate, but not extraordinary. For-

Instruments are easy to read and accurate. Ignition switch is conveniently located. Handlebars are extremely narrow and have very slight rise.

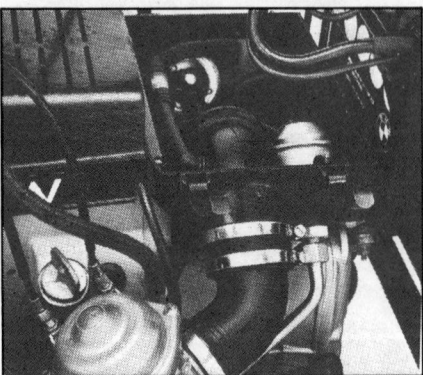
Plastic airbox contains easily changed flat paper filter. Steel tubes running from the airbox connect to the exhaust ports for emission control. Crankcase breather tubes run into intake tubes, which then drain oil into the carburetors.

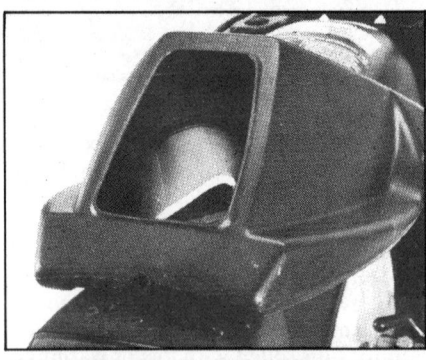
Storage bin under the seat is big enough for tools or gloves. There's a second storage area for the normal tool kit.

BMW calls this a sports cockpit. It is supposed to reduce front end lift and provide some wind protection for the rider. The protection is minimal and the plastic pieces wrap closely around the instruments so they can't be easily removed, but it does look good with the rest of the new styling touches.

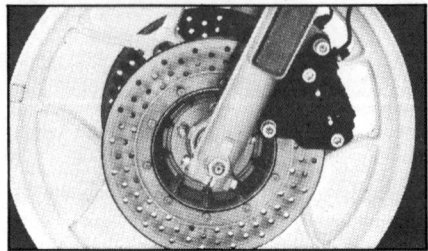
Double Brembo discs are used on the front of the LS, attached to new composite cast wheels. The brakes are powerful and controllable, the wheels attractive.

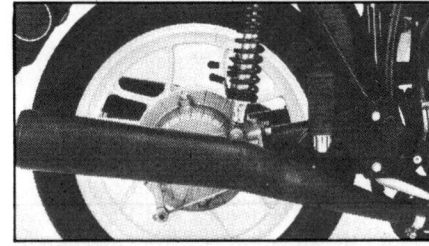
Mufflers are black painted and quiet. Single wall header tubes are lightweight. Rear spring preload is adjusted with lever permanently affixed to the shocks.

tunately there is still ample flywheel, so the machine can be accelerated from idle, in gear. Power is good, with quarter-mile performance of 13.99 sec. at 93.16 mph. That's substantially quicker than the 14.3 sec. quarter-mile time turned in by the original R65. Such performance figures may not cause much worry to owners of Japanese 650s who are interested in contests of speed, but it's fast enough to be clearly out of the commuter-scooter class of motorcycles. This is the most cammy BMW produced. It likes to be revved up to redline, rattling its little pushrods in excitement, while the rider enjoys one of the nicest shifting transmissions in motorcycling.

This has not always been the case. BMWs used to be famous for noisy shifts and marginal clutches. The R65LS is

blessed with one of the lightest pulling clutches anywhere. It is also positive and strong. The transmission is equally competent, shifting without noise or effort.

So what sort of a bike is the R65LS? Call it a lightweight sport bike for grownups. It has performance that doesn't show in quarter mile contests. It has handling that it doesn't get to use on racetracks. It has styling that everyone notices and, as far as we've seen, everyone approves of.

This may not be as uniformly fine a bike as the standard R65 is. The seating position is not for everyone. But the excitement of its styling added to the satisfaction of its handling and its air of quality make it perhaps BMW's most charming bike.

Yes, that's the word for the bike. It's charming. ◙

BMW NEWS
A Lightweight Sports-Touring R8OST is Added to the BMW Lineup for 1983

R 80 ST

N ew model announcements at BMW are always approached with speculation, owing to the long-standing rumors of a new four-cylinder model under development. So the big news this year is that the long-awaited BMW Four is another year away, and even next year it will be introduced in Europe before it's sold in the U.S.

In the meantime, the existing models have been shuffled somewhat, with two new 800cc versions of the traditional flat Twin added to the lineup. Most interesting of the two is the R80ST, a street-oriented version of the dual-purpose R80G/S. It keeps the solo rear shock and one sided swing arm, but with less wheel travel. The forks, a combination of R65 and R100 parts, also have less wheel travel, so the ST has a lower seat height. But it retains the high mounted exhaust. Tires are low profile street tires, a 19 in. front and 18 in. rear, mounted on attractive wire spoke wheels. Normal BMW instrumentation is included in the ST, and the seat has more padding than the G/S, along with the lower seat height.

The other new model is the R80RT, an economy full dresser, with the RT fairing from the R100 model, mounted on the standard 800cc BMW. The 800 version doesn't get the self adjusting shocks or some of the additional instruments from the 1000cc bike, resulting in a lower price.

Cost is a large part of the BMW story. Last year prices were reduced during the year. So even with a 2.8 percent price increase for the 1983 models, prices are lower this year than they were a year ago. They range from $3600 for the base R65 to $3900 for the R65LS, $4190 for the R80ST or G/S, $4990 for the R100 standard model, $6590 for the R100RS, $6990 for the R100RT and $5490 for the R80RT.

To back up the image of a better built

R 80 RT

motorcycle, BMW is now including a 36 month unlimited mileage warranty on all new motorcycles, including unsold 1982 models.

To make it easy to own a new BMW, a nationwide leasing plan is being offered through GE Credit. With the lease plan, it will be possible to ride a new BMW while spending less money.

When the new model is announced, BMW says the existing flat Twins will continue in the lineup. ◙

"the bike, she smiles at

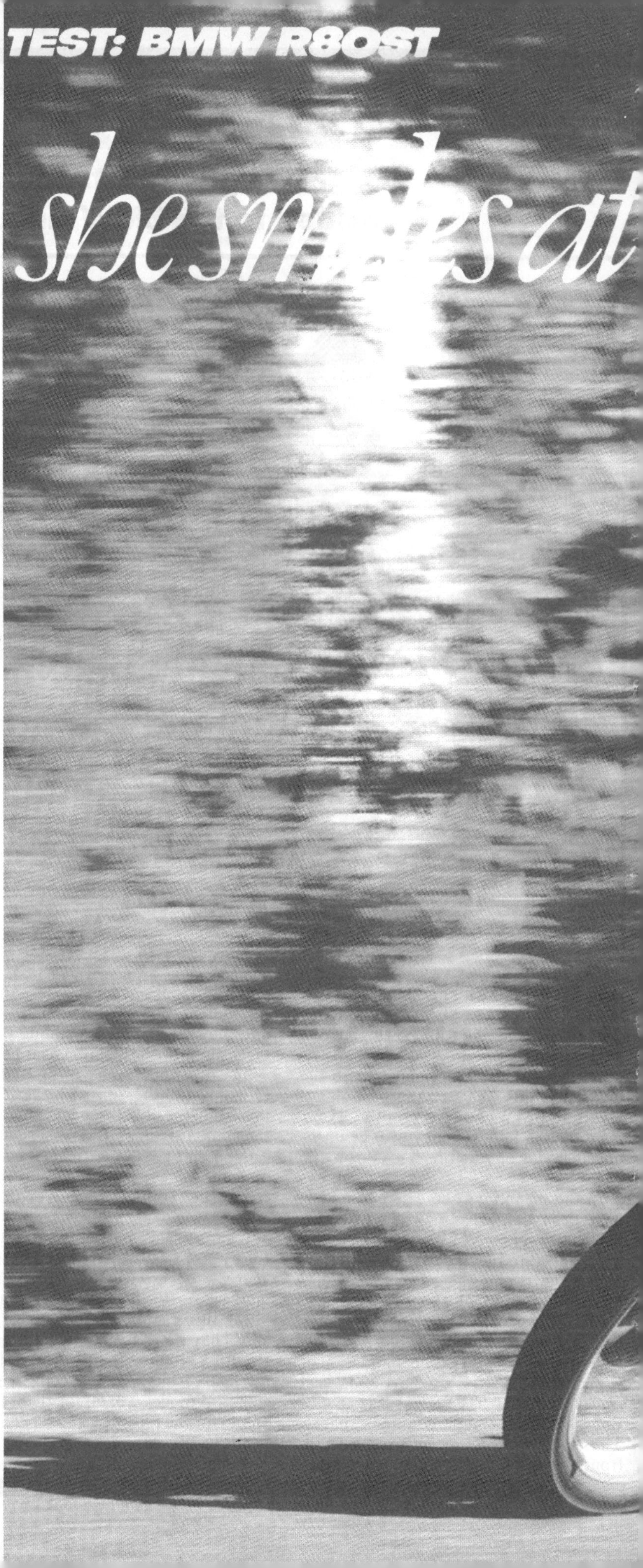

There are no new BMWs, a friend of ours once observed at the dawning of a new model year, only new numbers and letters, and maybe a new styling touch or two. This observation came toward the end of an exciting, two-hour discussion about all of the breathtaking new models that would soon fill showroom floors. For one hour and 58 min., we waxed enthusiastic over new engines, new frames, new suspensions, new styling—all-new bikes—that the Big Four manufacturers were dangling before us.

"What about BMWs?" a tentative voice asked during a pause. Silence. Then our friend stood up, pulled on his jacket, hefted his helmet, nodded wisely and uttered his pronouncement. There were few disagreements.

Truth of the matter was, giving in to indifference when discussing BMW was rather easy. It still is. Since 1923, the German make has meant, with a few exceptions, the same thing: opposed Twin engine, two valves per cylinder, pushrods, two carbs and a driveshaft. It's not a great leap from that to "There's no such thing as a new BMW." A BMW is a BMW is a BMW, right?

Wrong, and here's proof: BMW's R80 ST. Okay, it doesn't really qualify for the adjective "brand-new"; it's still steeped in the BMW tradition (see preceding paragraph) and it was born of the go-anywhere R80 G/S. But the R80 ST is so, well, pleasing to ride that it definitely deserves the NEW! IMPROVED! label.

First, a bit of not-so-distant history. In 1980, BMW introduced the R80 G/S, an almost-dual-purpose bike aimed at the exploring market. The G/S (the initials came from the German words for Woods/Street) had an 800cc engine, extra ground clearance, a single rear shock, a single-sided swing arm (which doubled as the drive shaft housing), and a high-rise 2-into-1 exhaust system. "All in all, a great machine for getting away from it all," we judged (*Cycle World*, April 1981).

The G/S sold reasonably well, but there seemed to be more interest in a street-only version. A BMW spokesman recently recalled: "We saw buyers converting the G/S to all-street bikes, and people kept asking where was the street R80." So, the ST—for Street Touring—was a natural.

Of course an 800cc street BMW is not, by itself, anything new. In 1978, BMW expanded the bore of the trusty R75 and created the original R80. At that time the R80 was sandwiched between the bigger and faster R100 models and a slower R60 model that subsequently disappeared and was succeeded by a more sporting R65 model. Somewhere along the line the R80 standard model>

me like a pretty girl."

The R80ST is a new version of a well-known bike. The lightweight pieces from the off-road G/S are at home on the road.

faded away when the G/S was introduced. It wasn't that a 800cc BMW was a bad idea, it just needed some kind of distinction from the larger BMWs. That's where the ST comes in.

Essentially, the ST is a G/S with a narrower mission, changes kept to a minimum. Only things which needed to be redesigned, were. What didn't need changing for the street, wasn't. That's in keeping with another BMW tradition: no change simply for change's sake. The ST got new wheels and tires, shorter forks and rear shock, more instrumentation, a slightly stronger battery, lower handlebars, an improved seat and a set of crash guards. Along the way, it lost the G/S's kick starter.

The engine is the 797.5cc ohv opposed Twin, a small-bore version of BMW's standard big Twin engine. Bore is 84.8mm. Stroke is 70.6mm, the same as that of the 1000cc boxer engines. Valve sizes are 42mm for the intake and 38mm for the exhaust; each is held open for 305°, a BMW standard. They're operated by pushrods and rocker arms. According to the company's rather peculiar way of putting it, the "maximum permissible engine speed" is 7400 rpm, while the "maximum continuous engine speed is 7200 rpm (as is the tachometer redline). Cylinders are aluminum, with a nickel/silicone-carbide coating. The compression ratio is 8.2:1. Carburetion is by a pair of 32mm Bing CVs. The exhaust pipes join in a collector box below the transmission; a single pipe then sweeps up to a shielded muffler mounted just beneath the seat. Ignition is electronically triggered.

The ST has a single-plate dry clutch with diaphragm spring, and a five-speed transmission. Final drive is (there's that tradition again) by shaft.

The welded-steel, double-cradle frame has widely spaced, giant, 1.25-in. round downtubes that bend under the engine and then curve up to join a single backbone. Steering head junctions are reinforced by extra tubes and gussets. The bolt-on rear subframe, made of smaller-diameter tubing, supports only the seat, rear fender and the muffler.

The right-mounted, cantilevered gas shock has three adjustments for spring preload. Damping is not adjustable. The top of the shock bolts to the main frame; the bottom bolts to the short, wide single-leg swing arm. The telescopic front forks are similar to those of the R65 models. Both the shock and forks have been shortened in the translation from G/S to ST. As a result, travel has been reduced: the ST has 6.9 in. of front travel (compared with the G/S's 8 in.) and 6 in. of rear travel (compared with 7 in.).

A 19-in. front wheel replaces the 21-incher of the G/S, while the 18-in. rear wheel is unchanged; both are spoked, with Akront aluminum rims. Gone are the Metzeler enduro tires. The ST comes with low-profile Metzelers (100/90H-19 Rille 16 up front, 120/90H-18 Perfect in back). Brakes remain the same: a single, fixed-caliper Brembo 10.2-in. drilled disc in front and a 7.9-in. single leading shoe rear drum.

Odds and ends: Instrumentation resides in a little plastic dash that covers the lower, narrower handlebars, and includes speedometer/odometer/trip odometer, tachometer, neutral indicator, high beam light, turn signal indicator and warning lights for generator output and oil pressure. The fork lock, separate from the ignition switch, is on the left side of the steering head. The throttle is a straight-pull Magura. A 16-amp–hour battery replaces the G/S's nine-amp–hour unit. There's a 60/55-watt halogen headlight. The flush-capped gas tank holds 5.5 gal., a half-gallon of that in reserve. The seat is narrower in front, with foam rubber replacing the old plastic foam, and lifts off with the push of a lockable button. A tool kit and tire-patching kit are under the seat; a tire pump is stored in the frame's backbone.

Time to ride.

The boxer engine, as always, fires right up. And, again as always, usually dies after a couple of thumps. More tradition. Using full choke and a slight twist of the throttle, it generally takes several firings to coax the Twin into life. And that's when the weather is warm. *Cold*, cold starts are even more precarious. Once the ST is running, you can back off the thumb lever to a click-stop (about three-quarters choke) and ride away. After a few blocks, the choke can be released and the engine settles down to a comfortable, quiet idle, about 950 rpm.

BMW doesn't make horsepower claims anymore, but the original 800cc engine produced 50 bhp for the low compression version. Adequate, but not especially powerful. Just for comparison's sake, the 90° V-Twin in Ducati's 600SL Pantah turns out 58 bhp—and that's an engine three-quarters the size of the ST's. That rather conservative amount of power is reflected in dragstrip performance figures. The R80 ST turned in a 13.80-sec. quarter-mile at 93.26 mph, and posted a half-mile top speed of 105 mph. That's performance that any given Japanese 650—and some 500s—can meet.

But dragstrip figures can be, if not exactly unfair, misleading when it comes to considering some bikes. BMW has not, in recent years, been a pretender to the performance throne. Like its companions in the BMW line-up, the ST isn't a motorcycle that will hurl you across the countryside like a land-locked ICBM. What it will do, is transport you, smoothly, steadily, dependably—even, one could say, classically. BMWs don't blur. They travel.

The ST is powered by BMW's tried-and-true 797.5cc ohv opposed Twin, wrapped in a welded-steel, double-cradle frame constructed of giant 1.25-in. round tubes. The exhaust pipes bend under the frame, where they join in a collector box. A single pipe then sweeps up to the high-mounted muffler. The sidestand, well, if you take away the word "stand," you'll get an idea how functional it is.

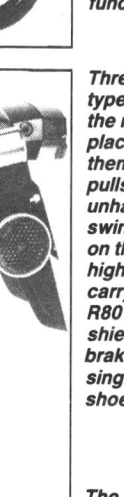

Three automotive-type lug nuts hold the rear wheel in place. Remove them, and the wheel pulls away easily, unhampered by swing arm or shock on the left side. The high-rise muffler, a carry-over from the R80 G/S, is well-shielded. The rear brake is a 7.9-in. single leading shoe drum.

The seat lifts off with the push of a button located on the rear fender. The button can be locked with the ignition key so the seat cannot be removed. Alas, the fork lock, located on the left side of the frame steering junction, is not so easy to use.

Rear suspension is by a right-mounted, cantilevered gas shock, which bolts to the main frame and the short, wide single-leg swing arm. The swing arm also serves as the driveshaft housing. According to BMW, the arrangement cuts weight and increases torsional rigidity.

The excellent BMW tool kit and tire-patching kit reside under the seat. Almost every common maintenance task imaginable can be performed using the tools that come with the ST. A tire pump hides in the frame's backbone tube.

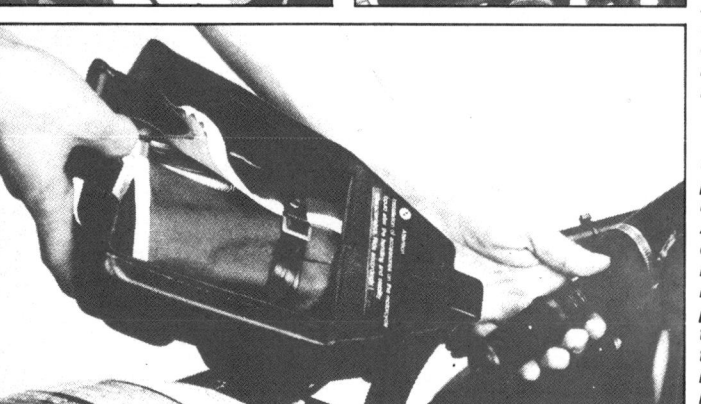

Cruising on the ST is a delight. The engine runs very well above 5000 rpm which, in fifth, will propel you along at extra-legal speeds. At that engine speed, the ST revs powerfully, without hesitation. Low rpm power is sufficient, but not abundant. Still, there's enough flywheel to keep things from being too balky; the engine pulls best from about 2000 rpm. Under hard acceleration, there's a flat spot from 4000–5000 rpm, but then, again, BMWs usually aren't pressed into that kind of service.

Clutch pull is light and the clutch is smooth, thanks to the diaphragm spring. The transmission shifts neatly and decisively through all five gears. The shift lever has a longer throw than that of many bikes, but you don't notice it after putting in a few miles. It's just matter of getting accustomed to the bike. One problem. Our test bike exhibited an occasional reluctance to shift from neutral to first while stopped. Slipping the clutch, or clutching a couple of times, remedied that.

On turns, the ST is responsive, steering quickly and lightly. The ST's agility attests to its light weight. With a half-tank of fuel the ST only weighs 432 lb. At highway speeds, steering slows some, but the bike is easily leaned over. And it's supremely stable, aided here by the low center of gravity provided by the engine configuration. Ground clearance (7.1 in.) is generous for a BMW. On a hard tack the brave rider will drag the pegs or the case guards, depending on the attitude of the bike at maximum lean.

Taut is the word that best describes the suspension. There's plenty of travel for chuckholes, mole-sized bumps and deep dips. But the stiff suspension doesn't absorb much of the jolt of small bumps such as highway expansion joints. Traveling over successive small bumps, the ST does a two-wheeled version of the jitterbug. Oh, and you quickly forget about the missing half of the swing arm. There's no sense of flex or imbalance. BMW says that the single leg and mounting point arrangement actually increases resistance to torsional flex.

An important note, although an oft-repeated one about BMWs. The rear end is quite responsive to driveshaft-induced torque reactions. Grab a bunch of throttle and the rear shock unloads; the rear end pushes up. Shut off the gas and the shock compresses; the rear end dips. Keeping the gas on while traveling over a pavement dip will tend to prevent the shock from absorbing the drop. If that happens when the bike is leaned over at the exit of a turn, the rear tire could slide. And closing the throttle while traveling over a bump will tend to prevent the shock from absorbing the rise. Under some conditions, that could cost you ground clearance you might wish you had.

The brakes work well, stopping the bike from 30 mph in 28 ft., and from 60 mph in 121 ft. That represents a major improvement over our 1981 G/S (which needed 36 ft. to stop from 30 mph, and 159 ft. to stop from 60 mph). The folks at BMW chalk the improvement up to a change in the composition of brake pads and shoes; the G/S had asbestos pads and shoes, while the ST has metallic ones. No doubt the street-only tires help

The ST is a pleasure to ride. The seat is firm, but not hard, and comfortable over a long distance. It's relatively flat, permitting easy movement. Passengers had no complaints. The seat, by the way, is high, a couple of shades over 33 in. That could present a problem for riders of average or small build.

There was a time when BMWs were considered virtually vibration-free, at least in comparison to other bikes. But now that many motorcycles have rubber-mounted engines (BMWs do not), they can no longer be said to be the smoothest bikes around. The ST is far from a shaker, but some vibration is noticeable, especially at low rpm when the engine firing pulses throb throughout the motorcycle. This diminishes to a light buzz, finally dying out at about 3800 rpm.

The lower, narrower bars felt good during both low-speed, in-town riding and high-speed interstate travel. Footpeg position seemed ideal, neither too far forward nor too far back. Shins occasionally encountered carbs, but that's the nature of a BMW and what're you going to do? The instruments are easy to read. The speedometer could be more accurate. When the speedometer read 60 mph, the bike's true speed was 55. And the controls aren't exactly placed in the most convenient locations. The horn button is too high on the left-hand pod. By the time you look to find the button and then accomplish the awkward thumb-stretch necessary to reach it, well, the reason you wanted to honk is usually far behind you. Once located, though, the horn is nice and loud. The kill switch is next to useless in an emergency. You can't operate it with your right hand in normal position on the grip.

Basic maintenance is a breeze. Single bolts fasten the two rocker arm covers. Valve lash is easily and quickly adjusted with everyday tools. Three automotive-type lug nuts hold the rear wheel in place. Remove them and the wheel slips right off. It's the most easily removed rear wheel ever. The word "excellent" doesn't do justice to the BMW tool kit. Almost every common maintenance task imaginable can be completed using the tools that come with the bike. Of the decreasing numbers of models that are sold tool-equipped, how many can boast that?

It's generally agreed that the finish, the detailing, of BMWs is among the best to be found on motorcycles. The ST

is no exception. The bike is available in two colors: a bright, screaming-for-attention red-with-just-a-dollop-of-orange, and a calm, conservative silver-graphite. Our test bike was red; the paint on the graceful gas tank was rich and deep. The frame was the blackest of blacks. The chrome was, hmm, *very* chromed. The finish is nothing short of elegant. Even the plastic fenders seemed, somehow, cultured; if there is a *creme de la creme* of plastic, this is it. The only thing that seems a bit out of character is the high-mounted muffler, but we grew to think of that as an endearing eccentricity.

The ST attracted a lot of attention, that's how stunning its appearance is. Kids stopped in crosswalks to compliment it. Women fawned over it. Old folks nodded friendly in its direction. Even the highway patrolman who stopped us for speeding was moved to deliver a rhapsody on the Beemer. As one beret-sporting gentleman with a foreign accent put it: "The bike, she smiles at me like a pretty girl."

Yes. Now a few nit-picks. There oughta be a law against BMW's one-minute-it's-there-the-next-minute-it's-gone sidestand. It has a hair-trigger spring that retracts it, as we put it in our G/S test, "as soon as you want, if not sooner." It's a public hazard. And don't even think about parking the ST head-first on a downgrade, no matter how slight, or on pavement that slopes to the starboard. You'll have some lifting to do. The locking gas cap will refuse to unscrew, permanently, if it's tightened too much. The fork lock is difficult to use, impossible to find in the dark unless you've had prior experience with Braille, and locks the front wheel in a position that contributes even more to the precariousness of the sidestand. And the bike comes with a silly folding key; you can't keep it on a keyring and it makes using the fork and seat locks even more of a maddening experience. Luckily, the spare is a normal key.

BMWs used to be not just expensive, but *expensive*, priced considerably higher than similar-displacement bikes made by other manufacturers. The gap has narrowed. A couple of years ago, BMW cut prices. Since then, they've gone up, but not as much as those of some of the other makes. At $4190, the R80 ST is almost priced competitively. And it comes with the longest warranty offered for a motorcycle—three years, unlimited mileage.

What you get for your money is a light, agile, uncomplicated, clean, attractive motorcycle. A bike that's refined, almost understated, not overbearing like some hell-for-leather machines.

Some bikes, you ride to travel like the wind, to get from Point A to Point B with the greatest of dispatch. The R80 ST, you ride for the simple thrill of riding. ▣

SPECIFICATIONS

GENERAL

List price	$4190
Importer	BMW of North America BMW Plaza Montvale, N.J. 07645
Customer service phone	(201) 573-2151
Warranty	3 years/unlimited mi.

CYCLE WORLD TEST: BMW R80ST

CHASSIS

Test weight (w/half-tank fuel)	432 lb.
Weight distribution front/rear, percent	48/52
Fuel capacity	5.5 gal.
Wheelbase	57.7 in.
Rake/trail	27.5°/4.9 in.
Handlebar width	28 in.
Seat height	33.4 in.
Seat width	8.5 in.
Footpeg height	13.6 in.
Ground clearance	8.0 in.
Headlight	60/55w halogen
GVWR	881 lb.
Load capacity	449 lb.

SUSPENSION/BRAKES/TIRES

Suspension:	
Front	telescopic forks
Travel	6.9 in.
Rear	swing arm, single shock
Travel	6.0 in.
Wheels:	
Front	1.85 x 19 in.
Rear	2.50 x 18 in.
Tires:	
Front	Metzler 100/90-19H Rille 16
Rear	Metzler 120/90-18H ME99A
Rear tire revs. per mi.	795
Brakes:	
Front	10.2 in. disc
Rear	7.9 in. drum
Brake swept area	104 sq. in.
Brake loading (160 lb. rider)	5.7 lb./sq.in.

ENGINE/GEARBOX

Engine	ohv opposed Twin
Bore x stroke	84.8 x 70.6mm
Displacement	797cc
Compression ratio	8.2:1
Carburetion	(2) 32mm Bing CV
Air filter	pleated paper
Ignition	transistorized inductive
Claimed power	na
Claimed torque	na
Lubrication	wet sump
Oil capacity	2.4 qt.
Electrical power	280w alternator
Starter	electric
Battery	12v 16ah
Primary drive	n.a.
Clutch	dry, single plate
Final drive	shaft

Gear ratios, overall:1	
5th	5.04
4th	5.61
3rd	6.96
2nd	9.61
1st	14.78

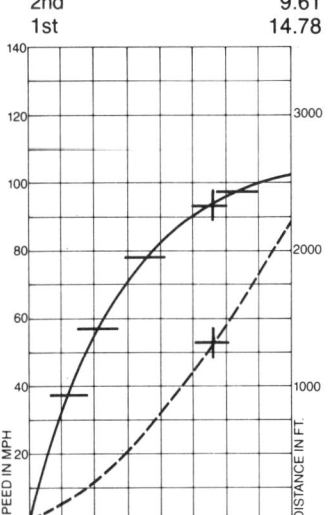

PERFORMANCE

ACCELERATION

Time to distance:	
¼ mi.	13.81 sec @ 93.26 mph

Time to speed, sec.	
0–30 mph	2.0
0–40 mph	3.2
0–50 mph	4.2
0–60 mph	5.6
0–70 mph	6.9
0–80 mph	9.4
0–90 mph	13.2

Top gear time to speed, sec.	
40–60 mph	5.1
60–80 mph	6.7

SPEED IN GEARS

Measured top speed in	
½ mi.	105 mph

Calculated at 7200 rpm redline:	
1st gear	37 mph
2nd	57 mph
3rd	78 mph
4th	97 mph
5th	108 mph

Engine speed at	
60 mph	4010 rpm

FUEL CONSUMPTION

Test loop	49 mpg
Range (to reserve)	243 mi.

BRAKING DISTANCE

from 30 mph	28 ft.
from 60 mph	121 ft.

SPEEDOMETER ERROR

30 mph indicated	26 mph
60 mph indicated	55 mph

If you had been building motorcycles with the same engine configuration for 60 years, you'd have to have a very good reason to change. For BMW, the reason was need. BMW needed to offer a flagship that would directly compete with Japanese motorcycles. That required a new engine, an engine with more power in a more compact package, an engine that would be smoother and quieter and meet all expected noise and emission regulations. BMW designers couldn't meet those goals with a flat Twin, so they designed a new Four as uniquely BMW as the opposed Twin.

The new K100 motorcycle was officially announced in Europe in September of 1983. The unfaired standard model went on sale at home a month later. RS (sport) models were scheduled to be at European dealers in December, and RT (touring) versions will be available in Europe early in 1984, but the K100 in any of its guises won't be sold in the U.S. until the fall of 1984.

The new design started with an idea: a broad powerband peaking at 90 bhp. The performance goals of the new model decided that long before the engine configuration was chosen. A four cylinder displacing 1000cc was a solution to the power requirements, but how should it be packaged to give the best all around motorcycle? Not like any other engine, was the BMW answer.

The crankshaft of the K100 runs north-south between the wheels, as does the crank of a BMW Twin or Gold Wing, but there the similarity ends. Imagine a Henderson inline Four water-cooled and brought up to modern standards of engine design. Rotate the top of the engine to the left until the cylinders lie parallel with the ground. Now slide the entire engine to the right until it's centered in the frame. That's how the K100 is laid out.

The advantages of this concept are that the engine is compact, easy to maintain, and has a low center of gravity. From the oil pan to the top (side?) of the cam covers is only 19 in. across, 8 in. narrower than a Gold Wing, and 10 in. narrower than a 1000cc BMW Twin. An engine width of 19 in. is more than competitive with most transverse Fours; only the ones with alternators carried up and behind the cylinders are narrower. Access to the engine is unexcelled. The valve covers and sparkplugs are out in the air on the left, removing the oil pan on the right exposes the crankshaft and connecting rods, and the cam chain can be changed by removing a cover at the front. In fact, a complete engine overhaul can be performed without removing the engine from the frame. Perhaps many motorcycle companies would prefer not to remind you of the eventual need of repairs, but BMW intends for this motorcycle to run for a good long time, and then be easy to fix when necessary.

Detail design of the engine lies somewhere between BMW automotive and Japanese motorcycle practice. Twin overhead camshafts are driven by a roller chain from the front of the crank. The cams operate the valves through bucket tappets, and valve adjustment is by changing shims. The intake and exhaust valves (one of each per cylinder) are set at an included angle of 38°, yielding a compact combustion chamber. Combine this compactness with the swirl-adding offset of the intake valve from the chamber centerline, and you have a quick burn engine designed to tolerate 10.2:1 compression ratio on low octane gas. Fuel delivery is by Bosch electronic injection, and spark timing is by a Bosch system that switches between two spark advance curves depending upon engine load. Both units are slightly simplified versions of fuel and spark controls used on BMW autos.

Bore and stroke are an undersquare 67 x 70mm; that's the first clue the engine was designed to be a 90 bhp unit throughout its life, without much room

A FOUR LIKE NO OTHER
BY STEVE ANDERSON
BMW DOES FOR THE INLINE FOUR WHAT IT DID FOR THE BOXER TWIN.

for future power increases. The 70mm stroke limits peak rpm to not much more than the current 8600 rpm redline. The second clue is the close spacing of cylinder bores. The all aluminum block is cast with siamesed cylinder walls, and bore centers are only 74 mm apart (the pistons run on a Nikasil-like cylinder coating; there wouldn't have been room for iron liners with this close bore spacing). The engine is a 1000, and it will never be made larger. The final clue is the engine weight: BMW has created a replacement for the 1000cc flat Twin that weighs the same but puts out an additonal 20 bhp. The BMW marketing decision was that 90 bhp was sufficient; their engineers have given them that power in a light, com-

pact package that won't easily yield more power to future tweaks.

A gear cut into the rearmost crank web drives a shaft under and to the left of the crank. This shaft goes forward to drive water and oil pumps, and aft to drive a large single plate dry clutch. Power passes through the clutch down a shaft with a spring loaded cam-and-ramp damper, and then through a gearset to the gearbox main shaft. After that it's through any one of the five transmission speeds to the countershaft and out the gearbox to the drive shaft. The gearbox mainshaft turns at less than engine speed, a situation that should improve shifting.

The drive shaft is unique in not having a heavy cam-and-ramp damper as fitted to other motorcycle final drives. Instead the front of the drive shaft is an aluminum tube, the rear is a steel shaft, and the two are connected by rubber blocks bonded to each where they overlap. Light, compact, and simple, the drive shaft is typical of BMW's efforts to keep this motorcycle light.

The engine, for example, is a large portion of the frame. The swing arm pivots from mounts located on the back of the gear box, and an open loop frame bolts to the engine/gearbox at five places to firmly tie the swing arm pivots to the steering head.

The frame is made of mostly straight tubes, and with the engine in place, the K100 must have one of the stiffer motorcycle chassis.

K100 forks use 41.3 mm stanchion tubes, forged aluminum triple clamps

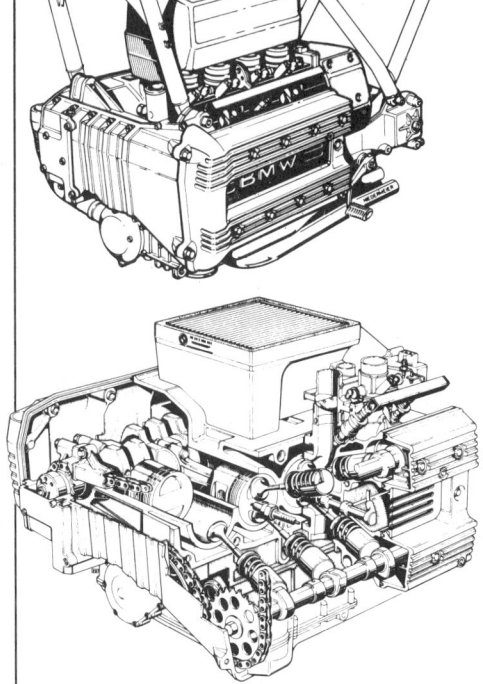

The engine forms an integral part of the frame. This feature helps stiffen the frame and keep the pounds off, but complicates vibration isolation.

There's little revolutionary about the engine except its orientation. The two-valve per cylinder Four puts out 90 bhp at the peak of a broad powerband.

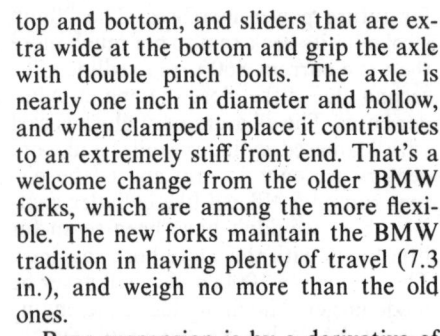

After 60 years of twins, the K100 is a new approach. Styling could be described as smoothed-out Katana, and the radiator grille emphasizes the BMW automobile connection.

The K100RT is a full-dress touring bike that weighs 543 lb. with half a tank of gas and should offer sport bike performance.

The new bike looks large and bulky until you park it next to the Twin. Then the smaller fairing and narrower engine of the K100 can be appreciated.

top and bottom, and sliders that are extra wide at the bottom and grip the axle with double pinch bolts. The axle is nearly one inch in diameter and hollow, and when clamped in place it contributes to an extremely stiff front end. That's a welcome change from the older BMW forks, which are among the more flexible. The new forks maintain the BMW tradition in having plenty of travel (7.3 in.), and weigh no more than the old ones.

Rear suspension is by a derivative of the single-sided swing arm first used on the R80GS. This time the swing arm is cast aluminum and connects to a single deCarbon type shock on the right side of the bike. Wheel travel is about 4.4 in., slightly less than used on previous BMWs. Concerned about swing arm flex with a single sided arm? BMW engineers assure us it isn't a problem, and the R80GS and ST have worked well.

When all these parts are put together into a motorcycle, it turns out to be extraordinarily light. The standard K100 weighs a claimed 510 lb. with half a tank of gas, the RS version 532 lb., and the RT 543 lb. Think of that— a water-cooled, 1000cc, shaft drive four cylinder touring bike, with full fairing and saddlebags, that weighs about the same as a sporting 750.

The shapes given to the K100 are clean and more than a little reminiscent of the Suzuki Katana. Which isn't too surprising as Hans Muth, the Katana's designer, came from the same BMW styling department as the K100's designers.

Even the unfaired model spent time in the wind tunnel, resulting in changes to the headlight pod. The faired models were thoroughly shaped by lessons learned in the tunnel, and the K100RS offers less drag and lift than the standard K100 while (according to BMW) maintaining the same amount of rider protection as the twin cylinder RS. The new RT fairing is larger and designed around higher and wider handlebars. Even so, it's claimed to have no more drag than the unfaired K100 with the rider sitting upright.

The K100 in metal appears more purposeful and compact than in photographs. The surprising thing is to park it next to a R100 Twin, and find that the new bike is the smaller of the two. There isn't a rough edge or thoughtlessly executed part on the K100; it looks functional and expensive, just as its designers intended.

Swing a leg over the K100, and the bike feels tall, as the 32 in. seat height might indicate. The pegs are further back than on other BMWs, and the bars on the standard K100 are a bend that leaned me forward slightly and placed my hands in a comfortable position. The bike fits well.

The instruments share a pod with the headlight, and consist of simple dial type tach and speedo. Digital displays are limited to a gear indicator and clock. There are the usual warning lights, and instead of a fuel gauge, there are lights that tell when the fuel supply is down to the last two gallons, and then the last one.

Switch gear is new and different, continuing a BMW tradition of innovative placement. These switches may start another tradition: innovative switch locations that are actually an improvement over standard layouts. Large buttons on the right and left switch clusters start the turn signal flashes. Push the right button down with your thumb, the right signal flashes. Ditto for the left button and signal. Unlike a Harley, though, you don't have to hold the button down. The signals flash at the first touch, and then self-cancel later. Or there's a button to cancel the flashing if you round a turn before the electronics give you credit.

The engine starts easily, the 'choke' control on the handlebars acts only as a fast idle position. Mixture enrichment is handled by the fuel injection. Blip the throttle, and the quick-revving Four tells you this is not your ordinary BMW. No torque reaction, either. The counter-rotating clutch and alternator cancel that, and the bike doesn't try to lean when the engine accelerates.

Accelerate is something the K100 does well. The engine makes solid 1000cc Four power, and the K100 hustles down the road like no BMW before. The clutch is light and positive, and the gearbox is superb, crunchless and quick shifting.

The power train, despite its exotic layout, invites comparisons. The exhaust note, and the gear noises coming from the engine, shout, 'inline Four.' So does the engine vibration which buzzes the footpegs at certain rpm. The engine character is a dead ringer for any number of Japanese Fours, at least those that are solidly mounted in their frames. Rubber mounted Fours are smoother running than the K100.

Steering is light and quick, very stable. The ride is well controlled without transmitting jarring forces to the rider. The front end dives under hard braking, but doesn't bottom. The bike builds confidence. Nothing drags except the footpegs during hard street riding, and even the dreaded shaft drive rise and fall is largely unnoticable.

Braking feels similarly good, at least in front. The front Brembo calipers offer good feel and stopping power without being too sensitive. The rear brake linkage has a block of rubber added to it, to help control a rear wheel chatter problem under hard braking. The brake feels, well, rubbery, and the chatter problem hasn't been entirely eliminated.

Over the 36 mile test loop BMW had set up in France, the unfaired K100 was most comfortable over the twisty, secondary road sections. On the Autoroute, the upright riding position was a pain at the 100 mph+ speeds that were possible. The aggressive sports fairing on the K100RS was the cure for that, and made life acceptable at the 135 mph speed the RS would indicate. There were drawbacks, however. The narrower bars on the RS increased steering effort, and the unique bi-plane spoiler fitted to the top of the windshield served only to increase helmet buffeting. Nor did the fairing live up to BMW's claim of matching the level of protection provided by the twin cylinder RS fairing. The new smaller fairing gives increased buffeting of the rider's arms, and hot air from the radiator heated the legs while riding the RS on the Autoroute; this wasn't the case with the standard K100.

The larger fairing of the RT looked as if it might eliminate the relatively minor shortcomings of the RS fairing, but unfortunately it wasn't available for test rides.

Availability may be the worst problem with the entire K100 series. None will be sold in the U.S. until the fall of 1984, then they'll be sold as 1985 models. BMW expects the price to be slightly higher than the comparable 1000cc Twins. That would put the standard K100 somewhere over the R100's $5300 tag, the K100RS over $6900, and the K100RT over $7400. U.S. models will come with slightly different fuel injection calibration, but no other engine changes. They'll also have a non-spring-loaded side stand, a feature deleted at the insistence of Jean-Pierre Bailby, who runs the BMW importing operation in the U.S. Thank you, Jean-Pierre.

The BMW model line up for the U.S. in 1984 is exactly the same as for 1983: the opposed Twin in 1000, 800, and 650cc displacements in the same range of street, sport, touring, and exploring models offered before. Devotees of the Twins have no reason to worry about the years after that. BMW envisions the Twin continuing in production indefinitely in displacements up to 800cc. Engine and chassis improvements are in the works as well, and future BMW Twins should reflect the lessons learned from the K100 project.

The K100 is an important motorcycle. It's an European bike that competes head on against the Japanese with no excuses. The K100 represents the corporate soul-searching that BMW went through during the late 1970s and the conclusion that came from it: BMW will never abandon the motorcycle. With the K100, there should be no need to. ◙

A BOLD NEW WAGER AGAINST THE VIRTUES OF TRADITION

If you fancy yourself a high-stakes gambler, consider what BMW has just done: wager 60 years of success with opposed-Twin motorcycles on the K100, an entirely new inline-Four. Now back that bet with a $110 million investment in development, tooling and the construction of a new factory as BMW just has, and the wager takes on proportions that are too rich for even a fat-cat Las Vegas gambler to handle.

There are those who will argue, and rightfully so, that BMW had to do *something*, that even though Max Friz's 60-year-old Boxermotor was most certainly a Good Thing, all good things must come to an end sometime. And for this Good >

SPECIFICATIONS

GENERAL

List price	$7200
Importer	BMW of North America
	BMW Plaza
	Montvale, N.J. 07645
Customer service phone	(201) 573-2151
Warranty	3 years, unlimited miles

CYCLE WORLD TEST: BMW K100RS

CHASSIS

Test weight (w/half-tank fuel)	546 lb.
Weight distribution front/rear, percent	47/53
Fuel capacity	5.8 gal.
Wheelbase	59.7 in.
Rake/trail	27.5°/3.9 in.
Handlebar width	24.0 in.
Seat height	31.9 in.
Seat width	11 in.
Footpeg height	13.3 in.
Ground clearance	6.9 in.
Headlight	55/60w halogen
GVWR	992 lb.
Load capacity	446 lb.

SUSPENSION/ BRAKES/TIRES

Suspension:		
Front		telescopic fork
travel		7.3 in.
Rear	single-shock swingarm	
travel		4.7 in.
Wheels:		
Front		2.5 x 18 in. cast
Rear		2.75 x 18 in. cast
Tires:		
Front		100/90V18 Metzeler
Rear		130/90V17 Metzeler
Rear tire rev. per mi.		790
Brakes:		
Front		dual 11 in. disc
Rear		11 in. disc
Brake swept area		253.3 in.
Brake loading (160 lb. rider)		2.8 lb./sq. in.

ENGINE/GEARBOX

Engine	dohc inline Four
Bore x stroke	67 x 70mm
Displacement	987cc
Compression ratio	10.2:1
Carburetion	Bosch fuel injection
Air filter	dry paper
Ignition	transistorized inductive
Claimed power	90 bhp @ 8000 rpm
Claimed torque	63.7 lb.-ft. @ 6000 rpm
Lubrication	wet sump
Oil capacity	3.8 qt.
Electrical power	460w. alternator
Starter	electric
Battery	12v 20ah
Primary drive	gear
Clutch	dry single plate
Final drive	shaft

Gear ratios, overall:1	
5th	4.71
4th	5.28
3rd	6.46
2nd	8.31
1st	12.64

PERFORMANCE

ACCELERATION

Time to distance:		
¼ mi.	12.56 @	107.20 mph

Time to speed, sec.	
0–30 mph	1.4
0–40 mph	2.2
0–50 mph	3.1
0–60 mph	3.9
0–70 mph	5.1
0–80 mph	6.5
0–90 mph	8.4
0–100 mph	10.8

Top gear time to speed, sec.	
40–60 mph	4.4
60–80 mph	4.2

SPEED IN GEARS

Measured top speed in ½ mi.	122 mph

Calculated at 8500 rpm redline:	
1st gear	51 mph
2nd	78 mph
3rd	100 mph
4th	122 mph
5th	137 mph

Engine speed at 60 mph	3720 rpm

FUEL CONSUMPTION

Test loop	39 mpg
Range (to reserve)	224 mi.

BRAKING DISTANCE

from 30 mph	32 ft.
from 60 mph	127 ft.

SPEEDOMETER ERROR

30 mph indicated	29 mph
60 mph indicated	59 mph

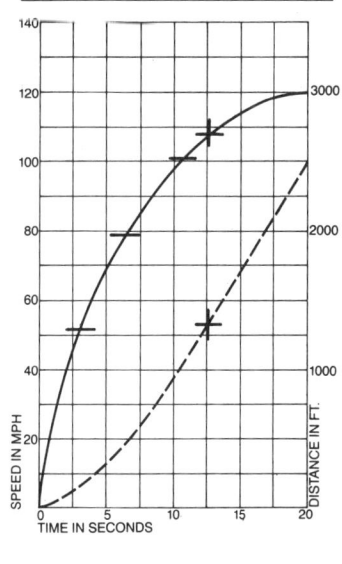

Thing, that sometime was not far off. The Twin already was laboring to pump out a meager 70 horsepower in its one-liter form, and upcoming noise and pollution regulations would have made maintaining even the present levels of performance more difficult than squeezing blood from a rock.

BMW, more than anyone, had seen the handwriting on the wall, so it stopped building the R100 models altogether, and has drastically cut the number of 650cc and 800cc Twins that will roll off the production line in the near future. The company's brand-new manufacturing facility in Berlin will produce 33,000 motorcycles this year—an increase of 20 percent over last year—22,000 of which will be K100 models: the standard, unfaired K100 ($5990), the sporty K100RS you see here ($7200), and the touring K100RT ($7500), all of which share the same basic engine and chassis.

What's even more chancy about BMW's gamble is that the company is playing a hand it dealt itself almost six years ago, back when the decision was first made to build the K100. At that time, the technocrats at BMW were charged with building a machine that would not only meet the projected per-

formance criteria of the Eighties, but one that would offer traditional BMW values—longevity, luxury, serviceability and, perhaps most important of all, exclusivity—in a market soon to be inundated with exotica from Japan.

Simply put, the Germans needed to build a machine that the Japanese would not. And in the quest for such individuality, many engine configurations were either tried or at least considered. V-types, square-Fours, far-fetched H-designs, even a horizontally opposed flat-Four was evaluated, although it was abandoned once it was deemed too similar to Honda's Gold Wing. Eventually, the decision was made to build a new machine powered by a dohc, liquid-cooled, fuel-

injected, one-liter inline-Four laid on its side with its crankshaft running longitudinally. And after making that commitment, the powers-that-be at BMW must have gnawed their fingernails to the quick as new engine designs from Japan started bombarding the marketplace all around them.

Luckily for BMW, there were no direct hits. And finally, after five years of development that included 10,000 hours of dyno time and 400,000 kilometers of test riding, the K100 became a production reality for the European market late last year. Now it's America's turn. And those who have feared that the precious essence of BMW would somehow be boiled away by the brewing of this new formula need worry no more. Because the most endearing of BMW qualities are present—indeed, maybe even *enhanced*—in the K100.

Now, understand that even though the K100RS tested here looks nothing at all like a Japanese bike and even less like its predecessor, the R100RS, it has been heavily influenced by both. The lazy lope

and subdued rumble of the flat-Twin engine have been replaced with a more urgent, higher-frequency whine, the same kind of four-cylinder song sung by the inline-Fours from the Orient; yet the bike still has the same air of dignity that marked the R100RS. It gobbles up highway miles in grand BMW style, but also can be snapped into and out of corners with a precision and surefootedness that no Boxer could ever match. It's a bike that can be herded along a twisty ribbon of road in the company of the best high-performance Japanese iron without losing its stately composure. So in effect, it's the best of both worlds.

There's no question that a really fast rider on a really competent Japanese sportbike can get from Point A to Point B on a winding road much faster than he could on a K100RS; but most everyone else can ride just as fast, if not *faster*, on the BMW while not working as hard in the process. The K100 has the kind of powerband, the kind of suspension and the kind of overall handling that simply make the fine art of riding quickly a whole lot easier.

There is no mystery about how the K100RS accomplishes this feat; BMW merely rethought and rearranged existing technology to fit within some new parameters. In fact, poking around in the RS's twin-cam, 987cc engine reveals

anything *but* cutting-edge hardware. The bore-and-stroke dimensions are unfashionably undersquare (67mm by 70mm, respectively), the cylinder head is of a bog-standard two-valve design, and valve adjustment is via the same type of shim-and-bucket arrangement that has been bumping poppet valves open for decades. Only the narrow, 38-degree included valve angle is in keeping with current trends in engine design.

But there's a good reason for all of the K100's apparent low-tech: It fits the requirements imposed by the use of a longitudinal, inline-Four engine of one-liter capacity. Were the cylinders any larger in diameter, the engine would have to be longer, for the bores already are marginally close together (9mm); and a longer engine would, in turn, mandate either a lengthier wheelbase (which is already quite long) or a shorter swingarm (which, if it were much shorter, would excessively amplify the up-and-down chassis-jacking caused by the shaft drive's torque-reaction). And since that more-or-less locked BMW into a small-bore, long-stroke engine (which is not conducive to high-rpm operation), a four-valve combustion chamber (which reaps its biggest benefits at higher rpm) made little sense.

On the other hand, the shim-and-bucket valve gear made *perfect* sense in the K100 engine. Not only does that arrangement meet BMW's requirements

Wind-tunnel test shows how the small, adjustable wing at the top of the RS's windscreen can be aimed to deflect the air according to rider preference.

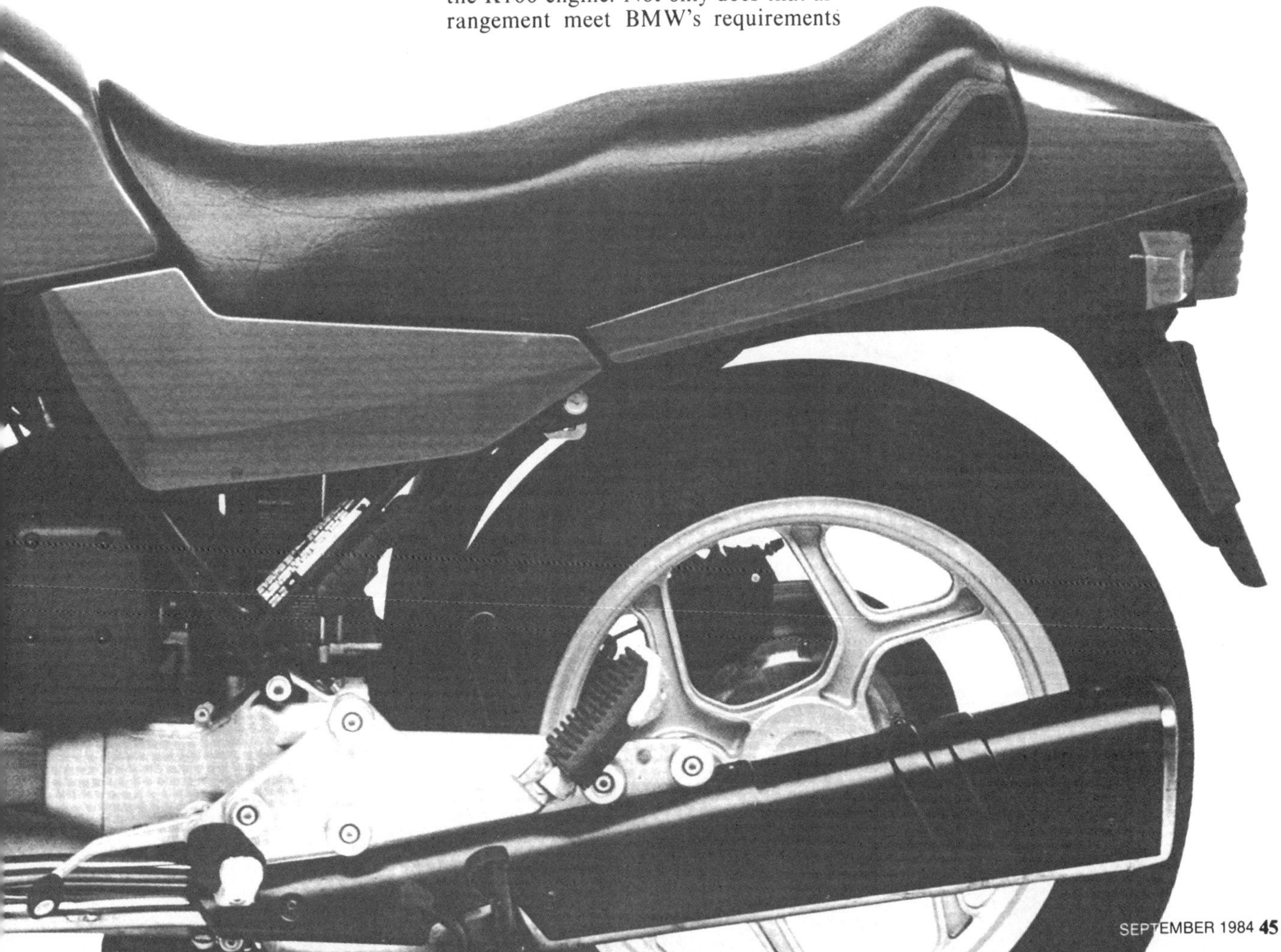

for simplicity and long intervals between adjustments, but it allows the camshafts and followers to be easily serviceable just by removing the cam cover on the left side of the motor. So, too, are the K-model's forged, one-piece crankshaft and its attendant plain bearings highly accessible, for they're all located just beneath the easy-to-remove aluminum cover at the right side of the engine.

Like late-model Boxer Twins, the K100 Four uses an electronically applied, nickel/silicon-carbide coating (called "Scanimet") on its aluminum cylinder bores, which are cast as a unit with the upper—er, left-side—engine case. Aside from being non-boreable, this coated surface is superior to a cast-iron liner in terms of thermal conductivity, plus it allows for closer bore-centers, and is lighter and more durable. Durability also was the prime reason for the use of liquid-cooling on the K100. And the fact that previous BMW motorcycles have been air-cooled was no drawback; the company has, after all, been building liquid-cooled BMW automobiles for a long, long time.

BMW's expertise with automobiles also was put to good use in the adaption of fuel injection to the K100. The bike incorporates a variation of the Bosch LE-Jetronic system used on numerous BMW cars for years. This system utilizes a black-box computer (under the RS's seat) that, through a series of sensors positioned in key locations in and around the engine, keeps tabs on engine speed and temperature, throttle position, and the air temperature and pressure within the intake tract. That information is analyzed by the computer, which then regulates accordingly the flow of fuel through the injector nozzle situated in each intake port. But that's all pretty much standard fare for a fuel-injected motorcycle, with one exception: On the K100, a Bosch-built electronic fuel pump is housed *inside* of the bike's 5.8-gallon aluminum tank as a part of a unique, completely sealed fuel system.

Bosch also supplied the K100's electronic ignition, which is tied into the injection system's computer box so it functions as both a performance aid and a rev-limiter. By comparing engine rpm with the amount of throttle opening, the ignition effectively selects one of two distinct advance curves to work most effectively with the load that's being placed on the engine. In addition, at 8650 rpm, which is just 100 rpm above redline, the ignition automatically retards the timing to deter over-revving. And should the rider ignore that first warning, the computer then shuts off the fuel-injection system altogether at 8750 rpm, and keeps it off until the engine speed drops back down to below 8750 rpm.

That fail-safe capacity is about the most sophisticated aspect of the K100's engine. But otherwise, the bike has an unremarkable, long-stroke, two-valve, relatively low-revving motor that fits right in with the performance program outlined by BMW's engineers right from the beginning: strong torque output at exceptionally low rpm, and a healthy if not spectacular peak horsepower production at only moderately high rpm. That's just what the K100RS has, too. The torque peak is at 6000 rpm, but the engine achieves 85 percent of that peak at 3500 rpm; and the claimed 90 horsepower is delivered at 8000 rpm, still well below the power peak for virtually all comparable Japanese engines.

What those numbers mean is that even though the K100RS isn't going to win any contests of speed with Japanese weaponry of equal displacement, the bike still is no slouch. Actually, it's faster than, say, a Suzuki GS850 shafty in just about every conceivable way, from an idling crawl to triple-digit speeds and everywhere in between. And it does that by producing the *kind* of power that is generally found only on something like a Honda Interceptor—smooth, uninterrupted, linear.

So no matter the situation, whether it's cruising the open highway or clipping along some remote country backroad at a classic sport-touring pace, the BMW always seems to offer you two, maybe three usable gears to choose from. And although the K100RS admittedly is no FJ1100-killing roadburner, it still romped through the quarter-mile in 12.56 seconds and 107.20 mph—not bad, considering that the RS has rather tall gearing, taller, even, than the standard K100's.

There's also an uncanny smoothness in the way the K100 reacts to changes in throttle. Off of idle in neutral, the engine seems to respond slowly, almost with a stumble. But when the bike is in gear and moving along, it offers a nearly perfect compromise between immediate response and gradual reaction. There's virtually no driveline snatch, no sudden lurches, no tendency to fall on its face, just a turbine-like outpouring of strong, steady power.

There is, however, a glitch or two in the K-bike's performance program, not the least of which is what seems like a rather fragile clutch. Indeed, in the middle of only the third run down the dragstrip, the single-plate dry clutch in our K100RS fried itself to a crisp. Then there's the matter of the vibration radiated by this new-wave BMW. Despite being rubber-mounted in the front, the engine buzzes noticeably more than a Japanese inline-Four of comparable size, and certainly more than any Boxer Twin ever managed on its worst day. It's a fairly high-frequency vibration, too, that is strongest right at about 55 mph in top gear, and it's felt most often through the footpegs. And the vibes didn't go unnoticed by the heat shield on the muffler, which self-destructed its front mounting

tab after only a few hundred miles of testing.

That's the sort of problem the Boxer never had; but by the same token, the K100RS doesn't pump up and down on its rear suspension the way the R100-series bikes did any time their throttles were opened and closed. And much of that improvement was wrought by what BMW has termed the Compact Drive System. In effect, the engine, the five-speed transmission and the unsprung mass of the Monolever rear suspension (a unique system using a single shock and a single-leg swingarm that pivots on the transmission case) are all one unit; and the rest of the bike—that is, the frame, with the bodywork and the front suspension attached—bolts to the engine unit and utilizes the engine as the main stressed frame member.

Other than being lighter and simpler, one reason why this arrangement functions so much better than the old design is that the center of the universal joint now is concentric with the swingarm pivot, whereas the two were about an inch and a half apart on the Boxer. On the old-style design, the driveshaft had to change length as the swingarm moved up

The one-sided swingarm greatly simplifies rear-wheel removal. Just pop off a small "hubcap" in the center of the wheel and unscrew the four lug bolts.

So that improvement, along with the use of three low-lash cushion mechanisms in the driveline (one spring-type cushion and two hard-rubber types) in place of the the two in the Boxer (both of the coil-spring variety), has eliminated most of the driveline freeplay that made riding the old bike smoothly such a chore. Gearchanging on the K-bikes is therefore not the least bit clunky or noisy, and off-on-off throttle transitions are not greeted with the lurching made

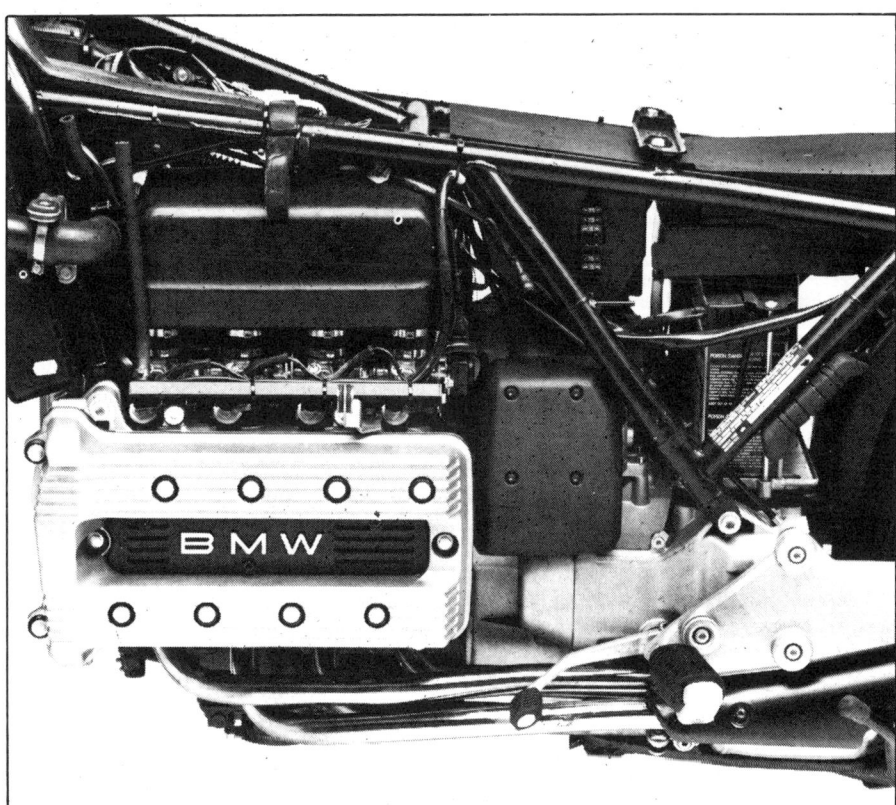
The entire engine/driveline unit, called the Compact Drive System by BMW, literally "hangs" from the frame and acts as the main stressed member of the chassis.

and down, which required a sliding-spline arrangement at the rear wheel. And the slip-fit tolerances of the splines simply added to the Boxer's already problematic driveline lash. But no such monkey-motion is required on the K-model, for its driveshaft remains the same length as the rear wheel moves up and down.

infamous by the R100 models.

Better yet, the K100 exhibits less of the up-and-down chassis-jacking that is always a concern on shaft-driven bikes. Some of that is due to the fact that the >

bike has slightly shorter suspension travel than the Boxer has, some is due to the fact that the rear suspension has stiffer spring rates with more preload and thus will not let the bike move up and down as dramatically. There still is a pronounced rise and fall, especially in the lower gears, but the problem is less exaggerated than it is on the R100 series.

Consequently, low-speed cornering in particular requires a bit of throttle-control to prevent excessive vertical chassis movement. But unlike the opposed-Twin BMWs, which often hammered their undercarriages into the road surface when the suspension compressed quickly, the K100RS has an abundance of cornering clearance in any case. The bike must be ridden *extremely* hard before first the footpegs, then the sidestand tang and the centerstand, graze the pavement. And even when something solid does smack the macadam, the RS remains unflinchingly stable.

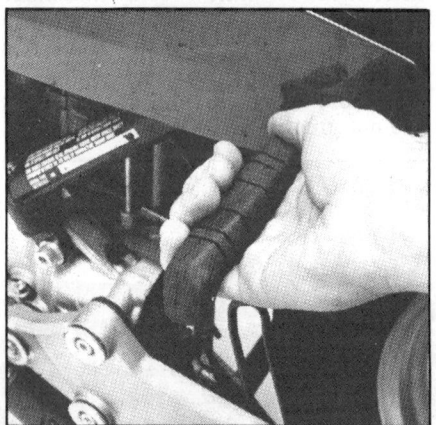

A retractable, rubber-covered handle swings out on the left side to be used as a lift point for rocking the K100 up onto its centerstand.

One reason why the bike displays such good road manners is its use of fairly sticky Metzeler Perfect tires, an 18-inch up front and a fat, 17-incher in the rear. Another is the rigidity of the front fork, a Fichtel&Sachs-built assembly using 41.4mm stanchion tubes held in place by thick aluminum triple-clamps. The fork also features a front axle that has a huge, 22mm diameter to maximize the rigidity of the entire assembly, and the axle also is offset 2.5mm to the rear to increase the trail a like amount.

That sturdy fork is equipped with two very powerful Brembo brake calipers pinching slotted, stainless-steel discs that are 285mm in diameter. The brake pads are semi-metallic and provide consistent, effective stopping ability in both wet and dry conditions. But although the front brake is powerful and requires only two-fingered actuation to slow the RS at moderate speed, it calls for a fistful of digits around the lever during high-speed braking. Despite its high-effort action, though, the front brake does not fade,

Traditional-style instrumentation includes LCD gear-position indicator (in tachometer face), low-fuel warning lights (one illuminates when 7 liters of fuel are remaining, the other at the 4-liter mark), and LCD digital clock that reads in military time.

even when used aggressively for long periods of time.

Not so the rear brake, which can be overheated with exceptionally hard use, sometimes badly enough to stop working altogether. And when used in combination with engine braking from fairly high rpm, the brake can also initiate some mild rear-wheel chatter, which is aided by the soft rates of springing and damping in the rear suspension.

BMW has always used long, soft suspension on its motorcycles, it seems; and although the K100RS has a tad less travel at both ends than the Boxer models of recent years, it is nonetheless plush, compliant and responsive to bumps of all sizes. The fork action is above reproach in just about every respect, with the possible exception of the dive it exhibits during severe braking. The fork offers no external adjustments, but the single rear shock has a ramp-type collar that allows the spring preload to be set at any one of three positions. At its lowest setting, the rear end is pleasantly supple on the highway, but compresses and moves around too much during aggressive cornering. At its highest setting, the shock is best-suited for hauling a passenger and a few days' worth of luggage. Thus the middle position is the most useful and versatile, offering above-average compliance, sufficient ride-height, and adequate resistance to bottoming.

And it is in those fast, sweeping corners where the K100RS really shines. Its suspension squats evenly and predictably as the apex is reached, and mid-turn corrections can be made with little effort. The bike is no featherweight, but it carries the bulk of its heft—which is the engine, primarily—in typical low BMW fashion. And so, despite its narrow, 24-inch-wide handlebar, the RS can be flicked into a corner or side-to-side quickly and easily. You'll never be tricked into believing that there's a 16-inch front wheel residing at the front; but with its steep (27.5-degree) steering head angle and short (3.9 inches) front

wheel trail, the RS is responsive and uncommonly neutral-feeling at all lean angles, even when braking in a turn.

It's easy to see, then, how a rider can lock himself into a smooth, relaxed, but extraordinarily *fast* rhythm on the K100RS without even trying hard. That's a fair description of sport-touring, an activity at which the RS performs brilliantly. The seating arrangement is better even than that of the fabled R100RS sport-tourer, for while the two are roughly equal in the swervery, comfort-wise, the K-bike is roomier and more luxurious for use on the open road.

The seat, for example, is padded with

The single-leg, single-shock swingarm uses massive aluminum castings to give the rear wheel at least as much torsional rigidity as a conventional two-leg swingarm.

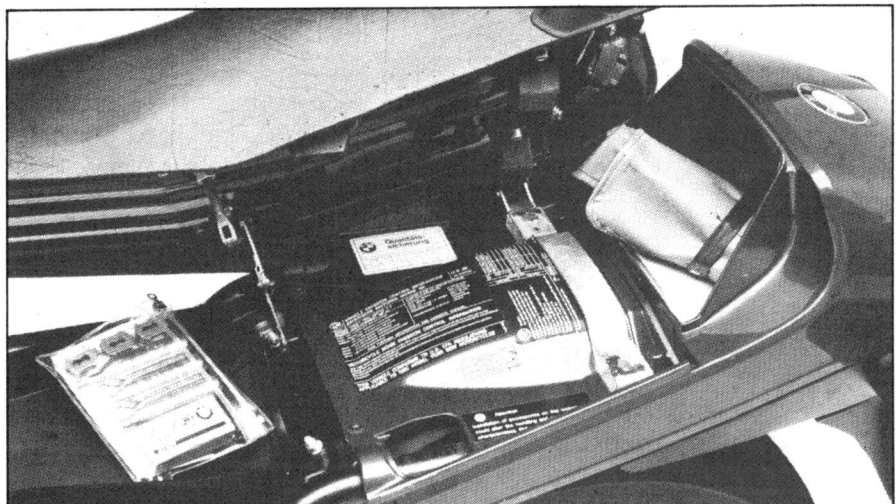

Just like on the Boxer models, the under-seat storage is plentiful. There's a large, covered tray under the front part of the seat, plus a spacious compartment in the tailpiece. Included is one of the world's great OEM toolkits, plus a complete tubeless-tire repair kit that even has CO_2 cartridges for inflation.

softer, thicker foam; and the footpegs have been moved back ever so slightly compared with those on the Boxer, which cants the rider a bit more forward and takes some of his upper-body weight off of his tailbone. And the low, narrow handlebar is designed to keep the rider tucked in behind the fairing so he's out of the airstream.

One interesting trick BMW employed to keep things calm behind the fairing is the use of an adjustable airfoil just at the top of the windscreen. The foil causes a venturi effect at the top of the screen, accelerating the flow of air back toward the rider's head. This little wing does not enlarge the envelope of still-air around the rider, but instead just smooths and directs the flow so that the air that does hit the rider's helmet is relatively free of turbulence.

We have no wind-tunnel numbers to substantiate our feelings about the aerodynamics, but we can attest to the fact that the fairing does an excellent job of protecting the rider. One of our testers got caught in a sudden downpour without his trusty rainsuit, but when he stopped he discovered that only his boots and the top of his helmet had gotten wet.

That's the kind of thing that can forever endear the K100RS to its owner. So too can a host of other well-thought-out niceties, such as: turnsignal housings on the fairing which snap off easily in the event of a tip-over; a taillight that can be popped off in seconds with no tools; an easily removable cam cover and crankcase cover that feature self-centering bolts and reusable rubber gaskets; a rear wheel that can be detached in minutes; and, of course, BMW's highly acclaimed toolkit, which can actually handle some major engine work, including crankshaft

removal. Then there are some real BMW breakthroughs, like a centerstand that is wide enough to provide stability when in use, and a centerstand that not only can be deployed from the saddle, but that won't retract unexpectedly and let the $7200 K100RS flop on it side.

What's more, the sidestand incorporates one of the slickest interlock devices ever to hit the market. The sidestand is linked to the clutch via a separate cable so that squeezing the clutch lever also automatically retracts the stand if the bike isn't resting on it. If it is, the clutch lever simply won't move. And since the

engine will not start in gear without the clutch disengaged, BMW has made it virtually impossible to ride away with the sidestand down.

BMW has also made it impossible for anyone, regardless of their allegiance, to ignore the new K100. The bike has already been voted motorcycle of the year in five European countries; in Germany

alone, BMW motorcycle sales have increased a staggering 120 percent since the introduction of the K100 last fall. And with the recent export of the entire K100 family to the U.S., BMW plans to increase its worldwide sales by more than 50 percent.

Ah, but to reach that sales goal, BMW figures that it will have to attract 35 percent of its K100 buyers from the ranks of Japanese-bike owners. And that's a sword that can cut both ways. Because should the K100 prove *too* successful, should this upstart motorcycle from Germany make any kind of a noticeable dent in the market-share of the Big Four manufacturers, you can bet your bottom Deustchmark on one thing: The Japanese will figure some way to flop an inline-Four on its side and put together a K100-clone that'll sell for thousands less. Maybe it won't be a *good* clone; maybe it won't take sport-touring to a new all-time high the way the K100RS has; but it'll *be* there, and the mere presence of a Japanese-built K100RS-replica could dilute the market for such a bike just enough to cause big problems for BMW.

We hope it doesn't come to that. We hope that the Japanese will ignore the

Access to the bottom-end components couldn't be easier. Just sit down next to the right side of the bike, undo the 10 bolts that secure the crankcase cover, and swing the cover outward.

small slice of the market that BMW might be able to capture and instead concentrate on bigger, more lucrative segments of the sport. We're willing to wager that they'll do just that. And so is BMW, obviously.

The difference is that we've got nothing riding on that wager. But BMW has bet the whole store on it. ◙

Prospecting on the world's weirdest dual-purpose bikes

GOOD AS GOLD

by David Edwards

THERE ARE SOME DAYS WHEN BEING ON A motorcycle is just about the grandest thing on earth. Days that make up for the traffic jams and the diesel fumes, that even the score for the cold hands, the sodden feet, the meandering Olds Delta 88s piloted by blue-haired kamikazes.

This was one of those grand days.

Cycle World's shop foreman, Bill Wolf, liberated from a week of sorting Allen wrenches, was leading, arcing a BMW R80 G/S through corner after corner, the bike's stuck-out cylinder heads barely skimming over the asphalt of California's Pacific Coast Highway. My front-row seat for all this backroad action was bolted to the frame of the rarest of dual-purpose birds—Honda's for-Europe-only XLV750R, a 749cc, shaft-drive V-Twin dappled in enough red, white and blue to be the center of attraction at anyone's Fourth of July parade.

We were 50 miles, an hour-and-a-half and one

> "All that's left of many mining towns are memories and bronze plaques."

sandwich stop out of San Francisco, on the first leg of a week-long loop of California's north country. We weren't making especially good time, which suited me just fine. I'd been on enough next-state-by-noon rides to know that I wanted this week to be different. I'd criss-crossed America any number of times, and all too often had been saddled with so many built-in timetables that all I'd seen of the countryside was a generic strip of arrow-straight concrete and billboards advising me that I had 17 miles to prepare myself for the next McDonald's. No way to tour on a motorcycle, especially bikes like the Honda and BMW, which don't have enough sense to stop when the road turns to gravel and then to dirt

That go-anywhere capability would come in handy, because this tour wasn't going to be hemmed in by yellow painted lines bordering a strip of asphalt. Northern California is bisected by a network of logging trails and dirt roads; pathways to isolated lakes, nearly forgotten cemeteries, deserted gold-mining sites and small towns populated by descendants of the fortune-seeking 'Forty-Niners. The best way to get back into the hills *and* enjoy the twisty roads that link the off-road attractions is on a dual-purpose bike; and with the 800 BMW and 750 XLV, we had the Mighty Joe Youngs of the street-trail world.

Getting ahold of the G/S was no problem; BMW has sold the bike in America since 1981, although it's been far from a best-seller. The XLV was another story. It seemed the only way to bag an XLV ride was a round-trip ticket to the Continent. Then we learned that a French gentleman had imported five XLVs to the U.S., and one was left. A rental fee was agreed upon, along with the stipulation that we replace any pranged bits, and the Honda was ours for a week.

I was working at not pranging any bits, as well as watching Bill dip the BMW around turns and congratulating myself for donning long underwear to fend off the early-autumn chill, when we streaked past an interesting-looking gas station. We didn't really need gas, but I wanted to stop anyway. I caught up to Bill and signaled that we should turn around. We idled up to the pumps at the Stewart's Point General Merchandise Store where the proprietor, Archer Richardson, was waiting, nozzle in hand. The Honda was closest.

"That's the most patriotic thing I've seen in weeks," Archer said, letting out a whistle.

As I pondered what could possibly

be more patriotic than the XLV, Archer topped off the bike's sculptured, 6.4-gallon fuel tank. In his 30s, tanned and with rugged features, Archer looked more like a rancher than your average gas-pump jockey. As it turned out, he *was* a rancher, with 60 head of Suffolk sheep grazing nearby on land that his family has owned for 100 years. Besides running the general store, Archer also had the town's sporting goods shop. When he found out we worked for a magazine, he suggested that we use his land overlooking the ocean for photos. "When you're done, I'll treat you to coffee inside," he offered, motioning to the warm-looking general store.

Soon enough we were bundled back up and on the highway headed for Mendocino, glad we had decided to stop, glad to be back on the road.

For motorcyclists, the Pacific Coast Highway north of San Francisco is a magical road. On one side, there's the angry blue-green ocean, rushing into the jagged coastline 100 feet below. On the other side, hills roll gently towards the horizon, dotted with sheep and cattle, gnarled cypress trees and weathered barns straining unsuccessfully against the wind. More often than not the landscape is cloaked by a wispy layer of fog that drapes itself over the trees and fills in the hollows between hills. The highway wanders through the middle of this storybook setting, its only purpose to move travelers a little farther along the coast, give 'em one hell of a view while doing so, and occasionally straighten out long enough to make room for a restaurant or inn. There may be more-perfect motorcycle roads, but I've not yet found them.

Upon Archer's recommendation, we checked into the Heritage House in Mendocino. Even though the romantic assemblage of 67 cottages overlooking an ocean cove is geared more toward honeymooners than two bikers in full enduro gear, we were soon warmly entrenched in one of its finer units. Bill and I rocketed out from beneath our down comforters the next morning, zipped through breakfast and were on the road by the ungodly hour of 10:30 a.m., headed for the first dirt roads of the trip.

Before venturing off-road, we stopped in the town of Leggett at Mabel Royce's combination gas station, supermarket, real-estate office and stray-dog sanctuary for a fill-up and quick snack. Mabel displayed the kind of spunk that the region's settlers must have had when they left families and homes back east for a shot at riches in California's hills: She had left a boyfriend and the "rat-race" of a San Francisco suburb, and had big plans up north. She half-jokingly referred to her modest facility as "Leggett Center Plaza" and gave us her view of the area's business climate: "There's plenty of opportunity up here, as long as you're willing to work for it," she lectured, before going on about her plans to re-open a tavern downtown. Have at 'em, Mabel.

From Mabel's place it was 12 miles to our turn-off into the dirt. If you're at all familiar with regular, single-cylinder dual-purpose motorcycles, then you know that they make wonderful streetbikes, especially on a twisty stretch of backroad. And in that regard both the more-powerful BMW and XLV were even better than we expected. The Honda, with its air-adjustable suspension front and rear, built-in fork brace and hell-for-strong front brake, was the easiest to ride fast, although getting situated behind that gigantic fuel tank—not unlike working the controls of a motorcycle while sitting behind a small desk—took some time. The BMW wasn't far behind, even though it was handicapped by less-than-stellar brakes and wheels shod with Michelin dual-purpose tires that were the knobbiest things this side of a motocross starting line. Besides carving impressive lines through turns, the bikes functioned well when the road straightened out and speeds picked up. Both bikes settled into an easy, 75-mph, big-Twin gait that other street-trail bikes, even 600cc Singles, couldn't hope to match.

I was worried, however, that because their performance was biased more toward the street, both bikes would quickly become unmanageable handfuls in the dirt. And then there was their weight. With its 5.15-gallon fuel tanked filled, the BMW was easily over 400 pounds, and the Honda had a claimed *dry* weight of 430 pounds; adding another 40 pounds of gas up high would make things really interesting.

As it turned out I was right, but it didn't matter much. The BMW was particularly frustrating, for every time I tried to plant my boot on the ground to steady the beast in a corner, I was rewarded by a soleful of aluminum cylinder head. Finally I resolved to keep my feet on the pegs and negotiate turns more slowly, with less slipping. Bill was using the same technique with the Honda: He *could* use his feet as outriggers, but the thought of dropping the rented XLV on its side and wiping out its expensive gas tank kept any Ricky Graham-replica slides at bay.

Still, we weren't out to set any speed records in the dirt, and as we bobbled our way toward Eureka, our slower pace allowed us to take in all the beauty of the surrounding straw-colored hills, isolated farm houses, grazing horses, swirling clouds and darting deer. Barrelling down a dirt road, ass-end hung out and in a cloud of dust, has its merits, but sightseeing isn't one of them.

After an afternoon of dirt roads, gravels roads and sometimes no roads at all, we pulled into Eureka, which despite its wonderful-sounding name, didn't look all that exciting. We checked into the Eureka Hotel, had a good meal in their restaurant, a great soak in their jacuzzi, and toddled off to bed, only to be greeted at 5:30 in the morning by the none-too-pleasant sound of rain splattering off the window panes.

"What do ya think?" asked Bill, probably hoping I'd suggest another four hours of sleep.

"I think we're going to get wet," I replied, trying to remember in which bag I'd packed my rainsuit.

After an hour of hopeful procrastination, we were headed southeast toward the old gold-mining towns of the Mother Lode Country, wrapped in protective layers of Day-Glo orange and canary yellow.

Northern California after the discovery of gold in 1848 must have been something to behold. It was the scene of the largest voluntary mass-migration in history as gold-crazed adventurers—argonauts, they were called—set up shantytowns of wood and canvas and tried to strike it rich. At first they panned and dredged in

the hundreds of streams and rivers in the area. Later, spurred on by hopes of finding gold-rich viens of ore, they burrowed miles into the ground. They even aimed high-pressure water cannons at the sides of hills and washed away tons and tons of dirt, trying to expose more gold, and causing so much ecological damage that the method was finally outlawed.

Today, most of the gold is gone, and all that's left of many of the mining towns are memories and bronze plaques. The more-established towns eventually got brick buldings, and many of those live on, if only as shells or foundations. But most of the clapboard structures were consumed by fire, and many that were spared that fate were torn down for lumber in the rationed days of World War II.

Still, there's a lot of history waiting in those hills and rivers if you're willing to go exploring. Which is just what we intended to do.

Our first stop was at Helena, just a quarter-mile off Highway 299. There's still a post office in Helena, housed in a two-story brick bulding built in the 1850s. The postmistress of Helena, a friendly, white-haired lady who looked to be old enough to have personally experienced a good deal of the town's history, gave us a rundown. Helena was named after the wife of the local brewer, probably a good example of the high regard the gold-seekers had for a good beer. There used to be an old hotel in town, but it burned to the ground about 10 years ago. Besides the post office, there's a livery stable, a couple of houses and the abandoned Meckle's Brewery, made of brick.

I asked the postmistress why Helena rated a post office. She looked a little hurt. "There're still quite a few people livin' in the hills around here. I've got a hundred boxes here and in the summertime most of 'em are used," she shot back, more than a little pride showing.

Fifty miles down the road, we pulled into Shasta, at one time the largest town in the area, the county seat, with 3000 residents. Shasta was a supply town that boasted the longest string of brick buildings north of San Francisco. As many as 1000 mules a week were driven into town to pick up food, clothes and mining gear. Today, a few brick walls, a museum and a park are the only reminders of the town's past glory.

Lunch and a 100-mile detour to see the Lassen Volcanic Park and its 10,500-foot peak had us hours away from the Kenton Mine Lodge, our destination for the day, with darkness approaching. We were on a dirt logging road, headed for Gibsonville, at one time a town of 500 founded in 1850 and deserted 30 years later when the gold ran out. We'd been warned at a gas station that there wasn't much there, which turned out to be true. All we could find was a sign and a pile of wood planks.

Since we still had 20 miles of dirt before we got back on a main road, we picked up the pace, with Bill leading and pulling away on the XLV. Our progress was impeded slightly by an empty logging truck with a would-be Jay Springsteen at the controls. Bill zipped past on a downhill but I got stuck behind the careening behemoth for a mile or two, the recipient of clouds of dust the thing was throwing up as it slid around corners.

Bill and I had read about the Kenton Mine Lodge in a guide to the historic inns of California and decided that it was the place for us. Part of one of the last working mining camps in California, the lodge buildings date back to the 1930s, although a group of Hawaiian prospectors originally settled in the area back in 1850. Lodge guests sleep in the bunkhouse or in one of the cabins that were used by the married miners; meals are served on long tables in the cookhouse. The entrance to the mine is across Kanaka Creek, with rubber boots provided if guests want to do a little spelunking in the mile-and-a-half-long shaft. Just up the creek is one of the few remaining stamp mills in the state, where ore was crushed so the gold could be extracted.

Since it was dark and we were still 25 miles from the lodge, Bill suggested we stop at a phone booth and tell the owners we were coming and to set aside a couple of dinner plates. All I got was a cold, impersonal voice informing me that at the tone the time would be 7:27. I dropped in another quarter and carefully guided my cold-numbed hands over the dial's numbers. Same voice, except now it was 7:28. "At least you can't say they didn't give you the time of day," said Bill, in his best line of the week.

We pressed on, along a wonderfully winding road, to the town of Alleghany and the turn-off to the lodge. Three miles of descending dirt road later we were welcomed by a strand of chain across the entrance to the lodge property. This didn't look good. Bypassing the chain, we rode up to the lighted cookhouse where two Labrador retrievers sounded our arrival. Two men soon emerged from the wooden building, thankfully without shotguns.

The men turned out to be Bill, who runs the Kenton, and his helper Doug. Bill made apologies for the place being closed, but the septic tank needed fixing, and he and Doug were taking a day or two off. "We're livin' here in God's country and haven't had a day off since May," he explained, "We're goin' fishing."

Instead of chasing us off, Bill invited us to warm up around the cookhouse's pot-bellied stove. He set a couple of beers on the table and explained his style of accomodations. "This isn't a Holiday Inn," he said, making a sweeping gesture around the authentically ramshackle room. "It's a country inn. It ain't fancy, but that's the way we like it."

With his faded jeans, lumberjack shirt and weathered face, it wouldn't be too hard to believe that Bill had spent all of his 30-odd years in the gold country, a descendant of some of the first sourdoughs to pan for gold. In fact, until two years ago Bill was a properly heeled maintenance engineer for the University of California at Berkeley's cyclotron, pulling down almost 60 grand a year. One day he got fed up with the house payments and the new car, and he and his wife pulled up stakes and headed for the mountains. You'd be hard-pressed to find a happier man.

Although Bill offered the use of his bunkhouse for the night, he suggested we stay at the Golden Eagle Inn in Alleghany, since his kitchen was shut down; and with the septic tank problem, restroom facilities would be a bit, er, rustic. He did invite us to come back in the morning and explore the mine while they were off fishing, offering to lock the biggest dog in the

cookhouse. "The other one won't hurt ya," he said. "We took her in to get spayed a while ago and I think they did a lobotomy at the same time."

After a self-guided tour of the Kenton Mine the next morning, we rode the 50 miles to Grass Valley and the Empire Mine State Park. In 1850, a lumberman named George Roberts discovered flecks of gold there in an outcropping of quartz. Roberts and other gold-seekers soon had the area pockmarked with a series of 20- to 40-foot-deep holes, but beyond that depth the going got too rough for simple hand tools. Roberts became discouraged and, in the bonehead deal of the century, sold his claim for $350. Over the next 100 years, the Empire became the largest hardrock mine in California, with 367 miles of tunnels carved into its rich quartz veins, some more than two miles deep. The interlocking system of tunnels was so extensive that burros were lowered into the ground soon after birth to spend their entire lives—20 or 30 years—pulling ore carts from one position to another. By the time mining ceased in 1956, $130 million in gold had been purged from Roberts' $350 claim.

The rest of our day was spent exploring the dirt roads around Grass Valley and Nevada City, two towns that sucessfully made the transition into the 20th century. There are plenty that didn't, though. We visited North Bloomfield, Relief Hill, Lake Bowman and Washington, but sadly, we didn't make it to French Corral, Rough and Ready, Timbuctoo or Yankee Jims. We talked to some of the people in the area, and discovered that there was still some gold to be found in the streambeds, but nobody was willing to admit just *how* much was there. "In the summer, people

make enough to get by," allowed one young man we drank a beer with. "But I've been here 15 years and I'm ready to get out."

We dined and slept that night at the National Hotel in Nevada City, the oldest continually operated hotel in the state, built in 1854 by a fellow with the unfortunate name of Zeno Philosopher Davis. During the heady days of the gold rush, the National had a gambling room and a bordello out back. Things are a little less invigorating these days: We settled for steak and a couple of beers in the bar before retiring.

Yet another lightning-quick exit and we were on the road by 11 the next morning, making for Sutter's Mill in Coloma, the place where the discovery of a 50-cent nugget of gold set off an explosion that would eventually see almost a billion dollars of the precious metal taken from the foothills and streams of the Sierras. On the way we stopped at the Miner's Club in Georgetown, a bar that served as a morgue at the time of the Civil War, where the bartender looked at us a little funny when we asked if there were any dirt roads in the area that led back to the highway. "Well, there's Mosquito Creek Road, but it's a lot longer that way." "Great," we said and jumped on the bikes.

By this time we'd gotten a lot more comfortable in the dirt with the bikes, enough so that we engaged in some impromptu wheelie contests, which, surprisingly, the BMW won, even if it did look ridiculous with its stubby cylinders pawing the air. And we even managed to string together some non-life-threatening slides, though berm-shots were still out of the question.

We'd toned our riding style down a bit by the time the parking lot of Gold Discovery State Park appeared on our left. There's a working replica of the sawmill that George Marshall was working on in 1848 when some gold flecks in a canal under the mill caught his eye. After we waded in the American River by the mill's original site, trying to catch our own gold flecks, we got on the bikes and headed for San Francisco, our week of playing latter-day argonauts almost over.

As we reluctantly glided back into the world of fast-food chains, billboards and interstates, I found myself repeating George Marshall's words on that historic day 136 years ago: "Boys," he said, probably holding his nugget high, "I believe I have found a gold mine." Remembering the people we'd met, places we'd seen and things we'd learned on this trip, I couldn't help but think the same thing. ◙

BMW K100RT

Can a Teutonic tourer find happiness in the Land of the Double Nickel?

THE $90 SPEEDING TICKET THE Arizona state trooper was scribbling out was almost worth it. For two days the BMW had been moribund on a seemingly endless slab of interstate, towed along in the wake of a horizon-hungry Honda Gold Wing. Then came the first genuinely twisty roads of the trip, and it finally was time for the K100RT to strut, time for the flat-Four Euro-tourer to skip ahead of its more-luxurious companion. It was time for fun.

Fortunately, the officer knew a little about having fun. Because after threatening to issue the speeding ticket, all he gave out was a written warning, along with a rather limp admonishment to keep the speed down a bit, delivered with a wink.

Ridden at the speeds it was designed for, the new BMW can be a ticket collector *par excellence*. Born on the speed-limitless autobahns of Germany and raised on the skewed roads that mow through the Black Forest, the K100 is a motorcycle that revels in motoring along with the ground blurring by at triple-digit speeds. It is a motorcycle that is very unhappy in 55-mph America.

Part of the reason for the bike's uneasiness on the radar-checked byways of this country is that BMW has failed to recalibrate the bike for America. It is essentially the same machine that prowls along Germany's high-speed roadways, and, as such, is in some ways overqualified for U.S. use. And, as we'll soon see, there are some nagging problems that remain unfixed from last year's introductory K100, problems that compromise the RT's effectiveness as an American tourer.

Not that BMW hasn't tried to give >

the RT more over-the-road appeal than the sporting RS model. There is a fuller, frame-mount fairing with extended lowers and a taller windshield. A wider, higher and more-pulled-back handlebar complements the new fairing. A redesigned, two-tiered saddle replaces the RS-model's flatter seat. BMW's plastic saddlebags, optional on the RS, are standard with the RT, and a matching tour trunk should be available later in the year. Also on the options-list are some interesting items, including fog lamps and heated handgrips, though, in keeping with BMW's rather Spartan approach to touring, you won't find such interstate-easing items as a radio-tape player or cruise control.

Mechanically, the RT is identical to the RS, with the exception of slightly reduced overall gearing, the better to cope with the the RT's two-up, loaded-down station in life. About the only other alteration is a rethinking of the stainless-steel muffler's heat-shield attaching devices, which had a nasty habit of breaking and rattling around. So instead of a leaf-spring attachment, the front mount now uses nylon locknuts, which BMW says are less affected by heat and vibration fatigue.

But while the heat shield may have made concessions to vibration, the footpegs still haven't. And this is perhaps the most disappointing aspect of the K100RT, especially since it comes from a company that for years has touted the importance of vibration control in its opposed-Twin lineup. Footpeg vibration was the major complaint about the RS we tested in our September, 1984, issue; if anything, the RT's footpegs vibrate more. The buzzing is particularly annoying between 55 and 70 mph, precisely the speeds that most Americans use while on tour. As velocities approach 100 mph, the bike's autobahn breeding comes into play again and the tingling diminishes, but traveling at that speed for extended periods is a sure way to kiss your license goodbye. The vibration imparts the RT with a coarse feel that is entirely out of place on a BMW, especially one with a $7500 price tag.

Though all four K100s that *Cycle World* has ridden have been afflicted with excess vibration, BMW officials say the condition isn't consistent throughout the entire K100 line. Still, they are aware of the problem and are about to release a footpeg kit designed to put the vibration complaints to rest. The kit will be available at no charge to K100 owners.

Another bothersome trait that surfaces during near-legal highway cruising is helmet buffeting produced by the double-lipped windshield, which sweeps back to within 12 inches of the rider's helmet, yet is low enough to look over. The double lip at the shield's top edge, similiar to the one on the RS but non-adjustable, is designed to accelerate air over the rider and leave him in a pocket of still air. It does not do a very successful job. As with the footpeg vibration, the buffeting is at its worst between 55 and 70 mph; and again, as speeds increase into the 90- to 100-mph range, the shield's effectiveness improves. Of course, the amount of buffeting felt at slower speeds depends on the rider's height, but judging by our test riders' comments, anyone

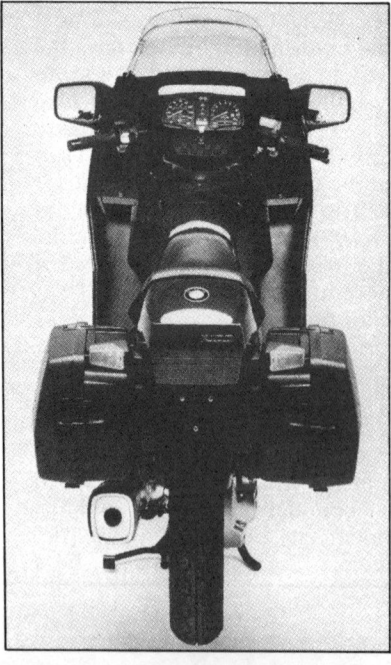

Touring European-style: The K100RT's distinctive fairing and clip-on saddlebags are world's away from the fuller fairings and integrated luggage of its Japanese and American counterparts. And so is the bike's weight. At 565 pounds, the BMW is more than 200 pounds lighter than a Honda Gold Wing, Yamaha Venture Royale or Harley-Davidson FLTC, and 300 pounds less than a Kawasaki Voyager.

taller than 5-foot-9 will feel the wind blast. Even tucking down behind the windscreen does no good, because the distortion caused by the double lips and the shield's extreme rake means that vision is seriously impaired.

The windshield's shortcomings are readily apparent because the rest of the fairing works so well. The fairing is very close to the rider, so there is little of the spillover effect that plagues many big touring rigs. Hand protection afforded by the mirror housings is especially impressive.

Vibration and windshield buffeting aside, though, the RT has some other, minor deficiencies that detract from the overall package. The engine emits an annoying gear whine, which is joined at idle by the whirring of the electric fuel pump mounted inside the aluminum 5.6-gallon fuel tank. Thankfully, both noises become less noticeable as speed increases. Although our time aboard the RT included a 1200-mile trek across Nevada, Utah and Arizona in 30- and 40-degree weather, it's apparent that in hot, humid climates the liquid-cooled engine could throw off enough heat to make a mid-town troll through snarled traffic an uncomfortable experience. And while the gray paint on the RT was better than the orange-peeley blue that our test RS was saddled with, it was still a notch below the excellent paint job applied to the Boxer Twins.

The RT's seating position also drew a small amount of flak. Because the seat is more sculptured than last year's version, it effectively locks the rider into one position. For most rides, the seat's padding, along with the comfortable handlebar bend, allows acceptably long distances to pass before a rest stop is required. On longer jaunts, such as an all-day drone along the interstate, a flatter, roomier seat would be appreciated.

If that list of criticisms seems debilitating, you should know that most complaints end where the interstate does. This is a bike for touring backroads, roads that meander over hills, across valleys and around mountains. It is on these roads that the K100RT leaves other touring bikes behind, where it gleefully takes revenge for the drubbing it receives on the interstates; where it has fun.

Certainly, the RT is no substitute for a hardcore canyon racer. It steers slowly compared to sportbikes with 16-inch front wheels, and the combination of a fairly short swingarm and shaft final drive makes for sloppy cornering if the throttle is indiscretionately whacked open or shut in mid-turn. Too, the excellent Brembo front brakes cause the front end to plummet during hard stops, a maneuver that doesn't bolster cornering confidence. So the BMW is definitely not a cut-and-thruster; but if you plan your moves deliberately, brake a tad early, concentrate on smoothness and keep cornering speeds up, the Beemer will fly. And more importantly, there isn't much drama to the fine art of cornering on the K100. Once set up for a turn, the bike will steadily arc its way through with little added input needed from the rider. And on twisty backroads whose paving is, shall we say, less than glass-smooth, the RT is a sheer delight to ride quickly, for it soaks up the bumps and stays on-line better than any other touring machine in existence. All in all, the RT is an easy, almost relaxing, motorcycle to go fast on.

Credit for the RT's rapid backroad canter goes to the suspension components and the engine. The front fork is a hell-for-stout setup that employs aluminum triple clamps, 41.4mm stanchion tubes and a huge axle. With the exception of sharp-edged bumps encountered at low and medium speeds, nothing upsets the non-adjustable fork unit. Controlling rear-wheel travel is a single shock, adjustable only for spring preload, mounted on BMW's unique one-sided swingarm. With a week's worth of luggage stowed in the saddlebags,>

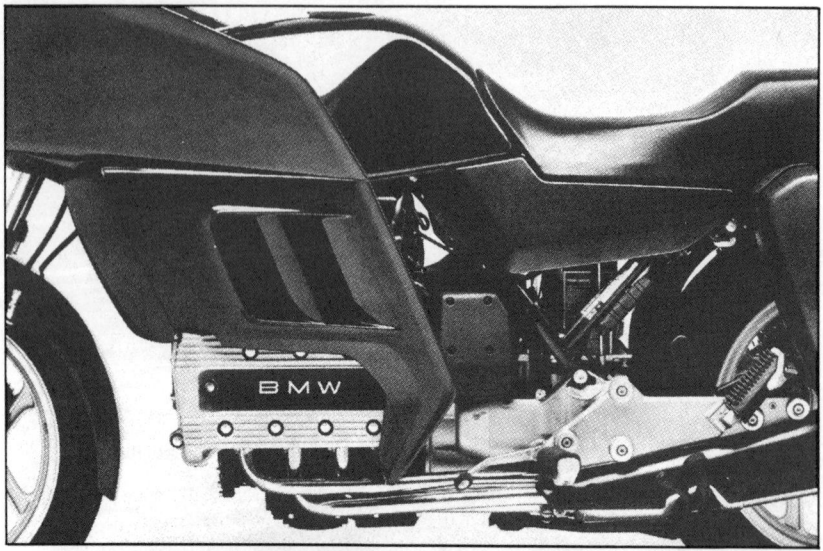

The BMW's laid-down Four won't shame a Japanese 1000cc sportbike in sheer acceleration, but its top-gear roll-on capabilities are impressive. A Gold Wing, for example, has to downshifted to third gear before it can get the jump on a K100 in 60-mph roll-ons, and even then the BMW soon pulls into the lead by virtue of its 7-mph advantage in top speed.

The RT's removable saddlebags attach to unobtrusive cast aluminum rails, and while the setup is secure, the bags can sometimes be difficult to re-attach. BMW sets the maximum load per saddlebag at 22 pounds.

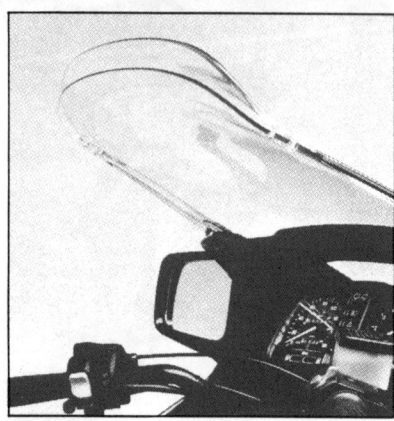

The K100RT's double-lipped windshield edge: a wind-tunnel wonder, perhaps, but not so good out on the interstates.

For riders weaned on Japanese machinery, the RT's hand controls, with push-buttons for each thumb, take some getting used to. Toggle switches on handlebar pad are *dummies, ready to accept accessory switches. The two fairing pockets are fairly deep and have enough room for gloves, maps and incidentals.*

the front and rear suspensions are balanced nicely. About the only handling glitch is a slight wallowing evident in fast, sweeping turns, say, at speeds above 80 mph.

Much has been written about the K100 engine being something of a technical underachiever. And with the exception of the laid-down configuration that gives the bike a remarkably low center of gravity, the long-stroke, twin-cam, two-valve-per-cylinder Four is not the stuff that SAE papers are written about. Still, there's no denying that the torquey powerplant works, and works well. With the Bosch fuel injectors delivering stumble-free performance and a wide-as-a-river powerband pulling the bike through corners seemingly regardless of the selected transmission ratio, the RT's 987cc engine is just one more thing the rider *doesn't* have to worry about during spirited backroad adventures. Matter of fact, the engine's outstanding mid-range power explains why the RT has an LCD digital gear indicator—something that BMW would normally term a "gadget"—inset into the speedometer face: The rider often *needs* it to determine what gear the RT is in while scooting along those secondary roads.

As entertaining as the K100RT is on those backroads, however, it's hard to escape the fact that touring in America often means touring on plumb-line-straight highways bristling with all manner of speed-checking devices. And here the BMW chafes. As evidenced by the retrofit footpeg kit, though, BMW seems intent on re-tailoring its new touring bike to better fit the American market. With better vibration control, a more reasonable windshield and some of the rough edges smoothed out, this motorcycle has the potential to be a best-of-both-worlds touring machine, one that would be able to reel off comfortable 800-mile days yet still capable of attacking in the mountain passes.

It would be shame to waste that kind of potential.

SPECIFICATIONS

GENERAL

List price	$7500
Importer	BMW of North America BMW Plaza Montvale NJ, 07645
Customer service phone	(201) 573-2151
Warranty	3 yr./unlimited mi.

CHASSIS

Weight:	
Tank empty	565 lb.
Tank full	600 lb.
Weight distribution, front/rear, percent:	
Tank empty	46.5/53.5
Tank full	47.0/53.0
Fuel capacity	5.6 gal.
Wheelbase	60.8 in.
Rake/trail	27.5°/3.9 in.
Handlebar width	27.3 in.
Seat height	32.0 in.
Ground clearance	6.1 in.
GVWR	992 lb.
Load capacity (tank full)	392 lb.

DRIVETRAIN

Engine	liquid-cooled, four-stroke, inline-Four
Bore x stroke	67.0 x 70.0mm
Displacement	987cc
Compression ratio	10.2:1
Claimed power	90 bhp @ 8000 rpm
Claimed torque	63.4 ft./lb. @ 6000 rpm
Valve train	dohc, two valves per cyl., shim adjustment
Valve adjustment interval	5000 mi.
Carburetion	Bosch fuel injection
Air filter	dry paper
Lubrication	wet sump
Oil capacity	3.8 qt.
Starter	electric
Electrical power	460w alternator
Battery	12v, 20ah
Headlight	60/55 halogen
Primary drive	gear
Clutch	single-plate, dry
Final drive	shaft
Gear ratios, overall:1	
5th	4.86
4th	5.47
3rd	6.69
2nd	8.61
1st	13.10

SUSPENSION/BRAKES/TIRES

Front suspension:	
Manufacturer	Fichtel&Sachs
Tube diameter	41.4mm
Wheel travel	6.8 in.
Adjustments	none
Rear suspension:	
Manufacturer	na
Type	single shock
Wheel travel	3.6 in.
Adjustments	spring preload
Wheels:	
Front	MT 2.50 x 18
Rear	MT 2.75 x 18
Tires:	
Front	100/90 V18, ME77 Metzeler Perfect
Rear	130/90 V18, ME99A Metzeler Perfect
Rear tire revs. per mi.	790
Brakes:	
Front	dual 11.0 in. disc
Rear	11.0 in. disc

PERFORMANCE

ACCELERATION

Time to distance:		
¼ mi.	12.74 sec. @ 104.89 mph	
Time to speed, sec.		
0–30 mph		1.7
0–40 mph		2.5
0–50 mph		3.3
0–60 mph		4.1
0–70 mph		5.3
0–80 mph		6.8
0–90 mph		8.8
0 100 mph		11.2
Top gear time to speed, sec.		
40–60 mph		5.1
60–80 mph		4.6

SPEED IN GEARS

Measured top speed	121 mph
Calculated at 8500 rpm redline:	
1st gear	49 mph
2nd	75 mph
3rd	97 mph
4th	118 mph
5th	133 mph
Engine speed at 60 mph	3840

FUEL CONSUMPTION

High/low/avg.	43/39/42 mpg
Avg. range inc. reserve	235 mi.

BRAKING DISTANCE

from 30 mph	33 ft.
from 60 mph	132 ft.

SPEEDOMETER ERROR

30 mph indicated	29 mph
60 mph indicated	57 mph

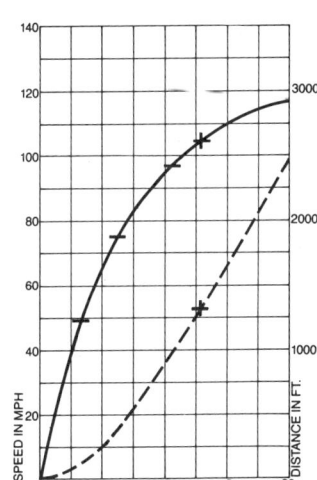

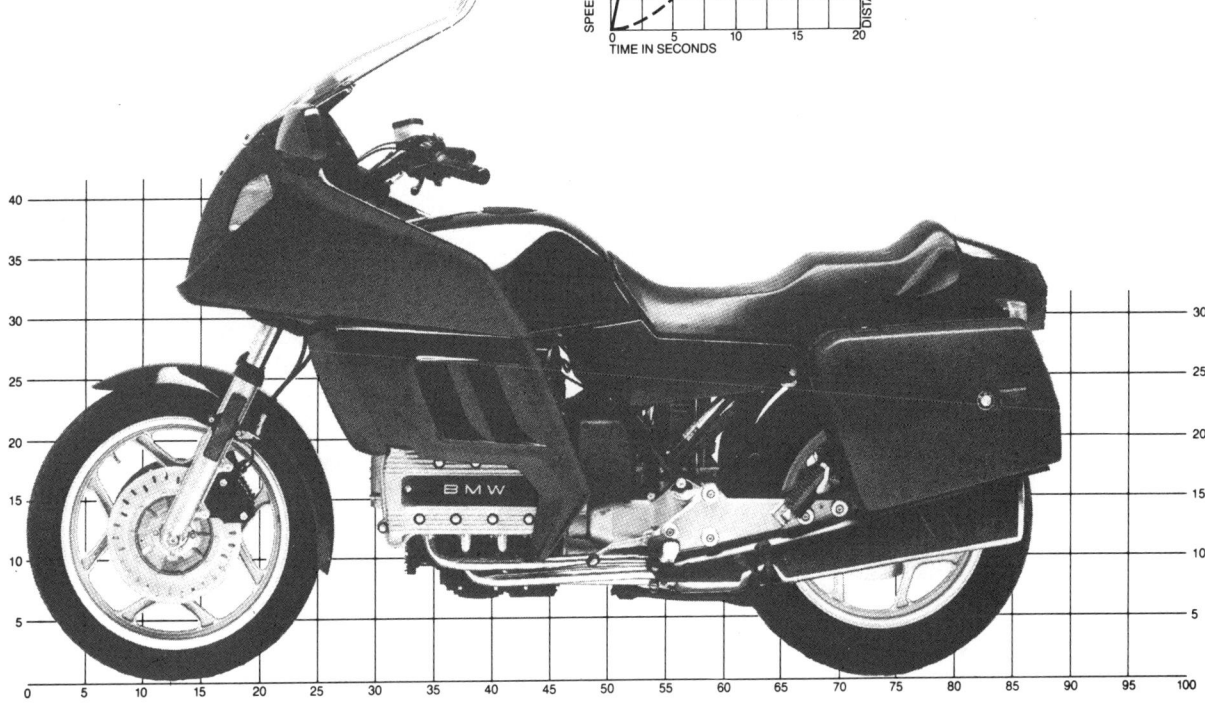

CYCLE WORLD TEST

BMW R8ORT

More beautiful after the honeymoon

M OST MODERN MOTORCYCLES seem designed to give instant gratification. You can sample their best qualities—their awesome power, their racer-like agility, their lightning-quick throttle response—in about as much time as it takes to run through the gears.

But not a BMW Boxer Twin. If your first ride on one of those is simply a quick buzz around the block, you'll undoubtedly come away remembering only the bike's worst characteristics, such as its lazy acceleration, its low-rpm vibration and its ultra-gushy suspension. A BMW Twin does have many endearing points, but learning about them generally takes time. Only after logging considerable mileage on the road aboard a Boxer does a rider begin to understand what the bike does best.

That's especially true with the R80RT. Not only is it one of those not-immediately-impressive opposed-Twins, it's also the smallest-displacement genuine touring bike on the market. Its 798cc engine makes only 50 claimed horsepower, yet it must propel a full-size bike that is almost as heavy as the model it supersedes—the 1000cc R100RT,

Even with a full fairing and bags, the RT maintains clean BMW lines. The finish is exceptional.

The luggage fits loosely on its bracketry, rattling and banging on every bump. But it is a snap to remove.

which itself was no ball of high-performance fire. So, the R80RT isn't going to knock anyone's socks off during a spin around the block.

On the other hand, this BMW has no competition. There is no other fully faired bike in the R80RT's price range or displacement category, so it fills a small niche in the market. It's a lower-priced, lighter-weight, mid-displacement alternative to the big touring rigs. The RT is devoid of all the gadgets that are standard on the Japanese-built tour bikes, but at $5700, it's also a couple of grand cheaper.

Mechanically, the R80RT is an interesting mix of old and new. Its overhead-valve engine is of the same basic design that has been powering BMWs

for more than half a century, while its chassis is built around the latest version of the company's unique Monolever single-shock rear suspension first used on the R80 G/S dual-purpose bike a few years ago. Much of the R80RT's bodywork has new shapes and contours, but the full-coverage touring fairing is the same as the one used on the R100RT.

There's not much different in the R80RT's engine, aside from new rocker-arm bearings designed to reduce valve-train noise. Our test bike seemed no quieter than previous BMWs we have ridden, however, so the effect of this refinement apparently is minimal. Same goes for the bike's new exhaust system. It's still a

2-into-2 arrangement, but with the crossover pipe now welded to the header pipes rather than bolted to them. BMW claims this makes the system 3 decibels quieter than its predecessor, while allowing slightly better engine performance and improved fuel economy. But again, our seat-of-the-pants dynos couldn't sense the difference.

Power-wise, the RT is typical BMW fare, in quality if not in quantity. The delivery is almost perfectly linear between idle and the 7400-rpm redline, with no flat spots anywhere. There's also no rush of acceleration anywhere, just a moderate, steady increase in speed. Really, though, in light of its heavy flywheels

and meager power output, and the fact that the RT weighs just under 500 pounds and has a fairly large frontal area, the R80 couldn't be expected to be a standout performer.

To help compensate for the RT's high weight-to-power ratio, BMW gave the bike 15-percent lower final-drive gearing than the R100RT's. That has, no doubt, done good things for acceleration, but it limits top speed to only about 100 mph. And while a touring bike doesn't really *need* to go any faster than that, this gearing causes the engine to turn about 4000 rpm at 60 mph. As a result, the nice, low-pitched engine *hummmmm* that can make open-road traveling on a BMW so soothing is not quite as low-pitched—and thus not as soothing. The R80RT's engine is still pleasant out on the highway, but it seems to be in much more of a hurry than the R100's ever was.

Also, because the R80 motor uses the same gearbox as the R100, that low final-drive gearing has moved the overall gear ratios quite a bit closer together. Fourth and fifth in particular now are so close that they don't make best use of the engine's wide powerband and decent mid-range torque. But at least the R80 changes gears more easily and quietly than BMWs of years past, although shifting still is a notchier, higher-effort activity than on most Japanese bikes.

On the positive side, that lower gearing does help the engine get up out of its vibration zone more quickly. When accelerating at lower revs, especially below 3000 rpm in the taller gears, the opposed-Twin engine causes the entire bike to shudder, sometimes so badly that you can't make out a thing in the fairing-mounted mirrors. But the engine smoothes out nicely by 4000 rpm, which makes cruising even at 55 mph virtually vibration-free.

Just as the engine is happier at higher speed, so, too, is the R80RT's chassis. Around town and during stop-and-go riding, the bike feels like a big, American luxury car with bagged-out shock absorbers. The front end dives radically during braking, and the whole chassis rises and falls dramatically as the throttle is rolled open and closed. There's not much you can easily do to change that behavior, either. The front fork has larger stanchion tubes this year and an integrated fork brace that minimizes front-end flex; but typical of BMWs, the fork is softly sprung and damped, and there are no provisions for any sort of adjustment. And the gas-charged Monolever rear shock—which attaches to the rear-axle housing as on the new K100 series rather than to the single-sided swingarm like on previous R80s—has only four spring-preload positions.

Out on tour, however, particularly over bumpy country roads and secondary routes, the R80's suspension defines the word "plush." The more you ride the BMW in that kind of environment, the more you appreci-

ate the way it soaks up all sorts of road irregularities without ever feeling the least bit harsh, despite the rather hard seat. But that's just one way in which the R80RT grows on you as you spend time on it.

Another is in its handling, which is better-suited to travel on the backroads than it is to cruising the interstates. Actually, the R80 deals with the latter quite well; it's just that riders conditioned to traveling on mobile entertainment centers are likely to find the BMW dead-boring on the open road, for it has none of the gadgetry that has made the Japanese-built touring rigs so popular.

But a ride through the mountains or on a long, winding country road is a different story. There, the R80RT is a sheer delight, for its comparatively light weight (about 300 pounds less than most American-style touring bikes), along with the exceptionally low center of gravity provided by the opposed-Twin engine, makes it the easiest-handling pure touring bike on the market. Because the single-shock R80RT is about 25 pounds lighter than the twin-shock R100RT, it's even more agile than its 1000cc predecessor. It can be flicked over into a corner quickly and easily, even during hard braking, and it allows a rider to move along a twisty piece of road at a spirited but controlled pace. It's easy to develop a nice, fluid, one- or two-gear backroad rhythm that is exhilarating yet non-tiring.

If you get too aggressive, though, the R80RT immediately lets you know that it's not a sportbike. A lot of engine-revving and gear-changing result in additional noise but not much else; the opposed-Twin simply doesn't have enough power to play sport racer. And even though the R80 seems to have a tad more cornering clearance than the twin-shock R100, the chassis responds to knee-dragging antics by gouging hardware into the pavement (especially if the throttle is snapped shut in mid-corner) and giving off a rear-end wallow that is just ferocious enough to discourage further aggressiveness.

The main culprit in that wallow seems to be the rear shock, which has insufficient rebound damping to deal with the rigors of full-blitz cornering. But it's hard to criticize the shock in light of the bike's touring mission—as well as the superb job the shock does of smoothing out even the most absurdly bumpy roads. It's one reason why the R80RT delivers its rider at his destination feeling less fatigued than he would on other motorcycles. Another of those reasons is the

63

A speedo, tach, voltmeter and clock are the standard instruments. The speedo and tach mount on the handlebar rather than on the fairing.

The BMW's Monolever rear-suspension system allows the rear wheel to removed merely by unscrewing four lug bolts.

The fairing incorporates a wind-tunnel-designed airfoil that enhances high-speed stability by creating downforce on the front wheel.

R80RT's full fairing, which offers rider-protection that is exemplary. You can ride the RT in a rainstorm and, if you're wearing a helmet and you keep moving faster than 30 or 40 mph, never get wet. In hot weather, though, the fairing is almost *too* protective; and the two little adjustable vents that flank the headlight don't pass enough air to make things any cooler for the rider.

Some riders will find a few aspects of the windshield displeasing, as well. For one thing, the view through the Plexiglas shield is extremely distorted; and for another, the shield is not tall enough to deflect the air over the helmet of a rider who is more than about 5-feet-9 in height. Whether or not those factors are bothersome depends upon the rider; some are willing to look through the shield just to

be fully protected, while others don't mind enduring a bit of helmet-level buffeting so they can have an unobstructed view *over* the shield. The latter group won't mind the R80RT's shield, but the former will undoubtedly hate it.

And if all R80RTs are like our test unit, just about everybody will despise the brakes. The rear brake is the same drum-type stopper BMWs have used over the last few years, while the twin-disc front brakes have new, larger-diameter rotors for '85; and the two systems work together to stop the bike quickly, predictably and easily. But in the process, both brakes give off enough squealing and howling to make every stop sound like a thousand fingernails scraping across the world's biggest blackboard.

It's also unlikely that anyone will

grow fond of the RT's sidestand, which is the same type of stand that has had BMW riders cursing for more than a decade. Not only is the stand extremely difficult to deploy while you're sitting on the seat, but it is spring-loaded to retract the instant most of the bike's weight is taken off of it. The company contends that this design is meant to keep anyone from riding off with the stand deployed, but there has to be a better solution. The centerstand has been redesigned to make getting the bike up on it much easier, but the sidestand still is a very expensive tip-over waiting for a chance to happen.

It's also difficult to understand the rationale behind certain aspects of the RT's detachable saddlebags. They do go on and off more quickly and easily than any other bags on the market, but they rattle loudly on their bracketry when empty or lightly loaded; they are so flimsy in construction that they distort when full and require some finagling to get closed; and they aren't particularly well-made. The bags get the job done, but they don't say "quality" the way so much of the rest of the bike does.

Nevertheless, despite all its numerous minor faults and major irritations, the R80RT is a competent, likable touring machine. And not just because it is the *only* touring machine in its size and price category. The RT could be the answer for riders who want just a hint of sport in their long-distance riding, who look·on a road map for the little black squiggly lines that lead them to their destinations instead of straight, red ones.

The only catch is that, as with most motorcycles, it's almost impossible to know if you like the bike until you first know what it does. And on the R80RT, that takes time. ◙

SPECIFICATIONS

GENERAL

List price	$5700
Importer	BMW of North America BMW Plaza Montvale, NJ 07645
Customer service phone	(201) 573-2000
Warranty	36 mo./unlimited mi.

ELECTRICAL

Electrical power	280w
Battery	12v, 20ah
Headlight	60/55w

CHASSIS

Weight:	
Tank empty	494 lb.
Tank full	527 lb.
Weight distribution, front/rear:	
Tank empty	46.2/53.8
Tank full	46.7/53.3
Fuel capacity	5.5 gal.
Wheelbase	54.4 in.
Rake/trail	28.0°/4.7 in.
Handlebar width	27.0 in.
Seat height (unladen)	31.6 in.
Ground clearance	4.9 in.
GVWR	970 lb.
Load capacity (tank full)	443 lb

DRIVETRAIN

Engine	air-cooled opposed-Twin
Bore x stroke	84.0 x 70.6mm
Displacement	797.5cc
Compression ratio	8.2:1
Claimed power	50 bhp @ 6500 rpm
Claimed torque	42 lb-ft. @ 4000 rpm
Valve train	ohv, two valves per cyl., threaded adjusters
Valve adjustment intervals	5000 mi.
Carburetion	(2) 32mm Bing
Air filter	dry paper
Lubrication	wet sump
Oil capacity	2.7 qt.
Starter	electric
Primary drive	helical gear
Clutch	single-plate, dry
Final drive	shaft

Gear ratios, overall:1	
1th	14.78
2th	9.61
3th	6.96
4rd	5.61
5nd	5.04

SUSPENSION/TIRES/BRAKES

Front suspension:	
Manufacturer	Fichtel & Sachs
Tube diameter	38.5mm
Wheel travel	6.6 in.
Adjustments	none

Rear suspension:	
Manufacturer	Boge
Type	single shock
Wheel travel	4.4 in.
Adjustments	preload

Wheel:	
Front	MT 2.50 x 18
Rear	MT 2.50 x 18

Tires:	
Front	90/90-18 Metzeler Perfect ME11
Rear	120/90-18 Metzeler Perfect ME99
Rear tire rev. per mi	792

Brakes:	
Front	(2) 11.2 in. disc
Rear	7.9 in drum

PERFORMANCE

ACCELERATION

Time to distance:	
¼ mi.	14.32 sec @ 89.73 mph

Time to speed, sec.	
0-30	1.7
0-40	2.6
0-50	3.9
0-60	5.3
0-70	7.3
0-80	10.1
0-90	14.4

Top gear time to speed, sec.	
40-60	4.8
60-80	7.5

SPEED IN GEARS

Measured top speed	103 mph

Calculated at 7250 rpm redline	
1st gear	37 mph
2nd gear	57 mph
3rd gear	79 mph
4th gear	98 mph
5th gear	109 mph

Engine speed at	
60 mph	3990 rpm

FUEL MILEAGE

High/low/avg	57/45/49 mpg
Avg. range inc. reserve	225 mi.

BRAKING DISTANCE

from 30 mph	30 ft.
from 60 mph	137 ft.

SPEEDOMETER ERROR

30 mph indicated	28 mph
60 mph indicated	55 mph

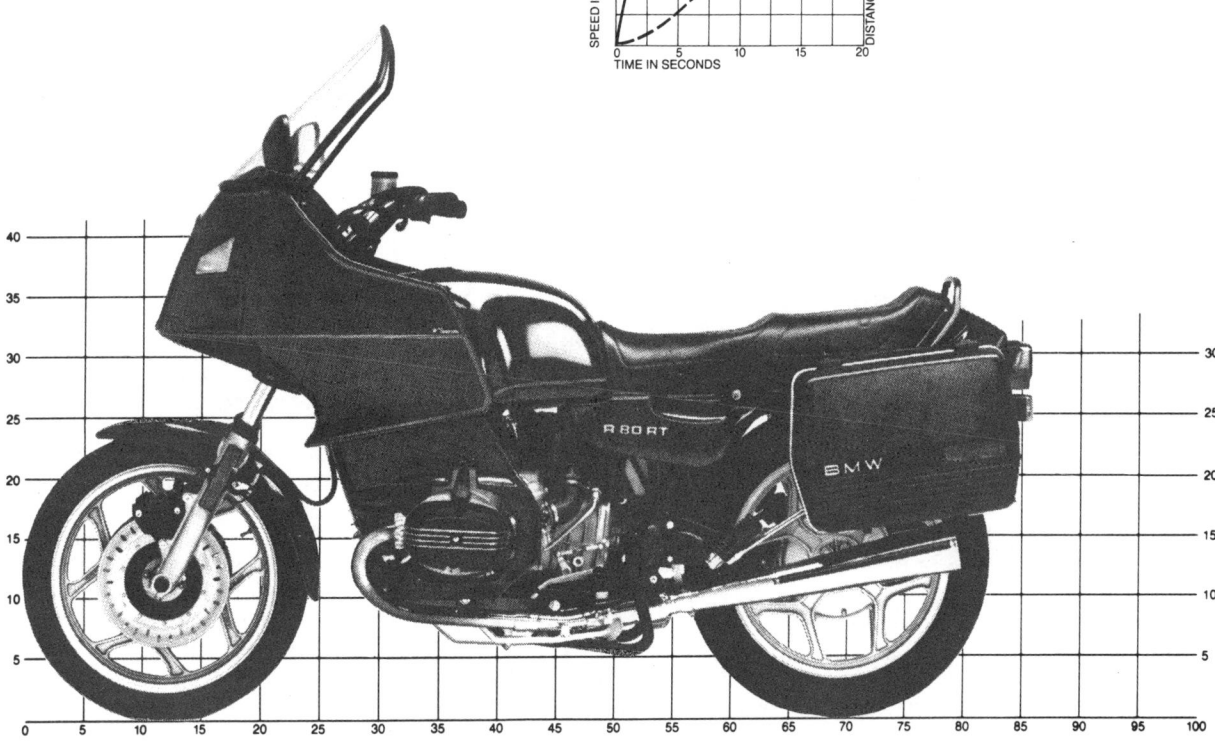

DISTANT RIDES

The world was a different place 25 years ago, but touring was no less fun

"TO HELL WITH THIS," MY friend Duncan Spencer announced one rainy night as we labored over his defunct motorcycle. "Why don't we fly to Germany and buy two *new* BMWs and see what it's like to go somewhere without breaking down?" With that simple roadside plea, Duncan planted the seed for a summerlong ride in Europe, a heady continental rush that even today, 25 years later, still evokes smiles and fond memories.

Duncan and I were classmates at Yale, which in the late Fifties was still a peaceful place, unwracked by the wave of student unrest that was to sweep the country a few years later. Still, there were causes to fight for, and ours was the university's ban on motorcycles, an unjust rule that we

BY GEORGE CADWALADER

circumvented by keeping our bikes in the garage of the university chaplain. As far as I know, the chaplain had no particular interest in motorcycles, but he was a bit of a rebel, and we gave him a chance to thumb his nose at the establishment while he gave us a place out of the rain, so everybody was happy with the arrangement.

As befitted revolutionaries, we operated with a pretty motley assortment of equipment. Jim Brewster rode a hot little Ducati Single, and Duncan had a usually inert piece of iron he called the "Mighty Horex," a name that had more to do with wishful thinking than fact. Flagship of the fleet was a giant old Indian that belonged jointly to my roommate, Bill Hunt, and Peter Beard, who has since gone on to prominence as a jet-set photographer. My machine (we

spoke of "machines" in deference to the English who then dominated the sport) was a tired 250cc Zundapp two-stroke Single.

Two hundred and fifty ccs in the days of my Zundapp wouldn't do what 250cc will do today. My frequent commutes up and down the Jersey Turnpike were exercises in patience until I learned to look for overtaking semis in my furiously vibrating mirror. Then I'd call on all of my Zundapp's 15 horses and, if I timed it right, I could get enough steam up by the time the truck went by to duck into his slipstream for a tow. This worked well enough until a near-miss behind a Mack with no brake lights set me to thinking about a bigger, more powerful machine.

But I had to make do with my Zundapp until a summer of slinging

hay bales put me far enough ahead that I even dared pay a visit to that then-Mecca of riders, Ghost Motorcycles of Port Washington, New York. There I found the old, but immaculately maintained, BMW R51/3 that was to carry me many thousands of miles in the following two years.

Many of the trips I made were in company with my friend Duncan who remained stubbornly loyal to his collapsing Horex. Occasionally I would borrow Bill Hunt's Indian as a respite from the stolidly dependable BMW, and Duncan and I would sputter and roar off on various excursions that usually landed us broken-down in far-off places where old-timers in parts departments vaguely remembered Indians and nobody anywhere had ever heard of Horex.

After a year or so of these increasingly frequent unscheduled stops, Duncan's patience with the Horex finally began to wear thin, and he uttered the words that would send us to Europe for two brand-spanking-new BMWs. The only problem was that I had signed up for a previous engagement that summer. Luckily, the Powers in Washington, D.C., decided that the Russians could be held in check without my help until the following September when I was to report for duty in the Marine Corps.

Butler & Smith, BMW's United States agent at that time, arranged for us to pick up two new R50s at the factory in Munich for what I recall was $600 each, payable in New York, while an obscure airline contracted to fly us to England and back for another $300 each. This didn't leave us with a whole lot of cash to eat with, but we figured we'd make out all right if we camped whenever we could.

Upon our arrival in Munich, we were met by a politely efficient BMW representative who showed us through the newly built plant where motorcycles and sports sedans rolled off modern assembly lines with Prussian precision. But behind this monument to Germany's industrial rebirth there stood a group of ramshackle wood-frame buildings in which craftsmen continued to build magnificent BMW limousines just as they had always done, entirely by hand. It was plain enough, even to a skeptic like Duncan, that the company's commitment to high quality was not simply an advertising slogan.

This impression was confirmed when two uniformed attendants wheeled our already warmed-up bikes into the sunlight, inspected them one last time for microscopic imperfections, clicked their heels and departed. We departed as well, stopping briefly at the nearby shop of the famous pre-war BMW factory rider, George Meier, before heading off for the lakeside town of Starnberg—where, we were told, Munich's single girls went looking for excitement.

Sadly, instead of spending that night in the arms of maidens, we spent it in a swamp. One of the pitfalls of traveling through Bavaria is that every little village has an ancient inn, each one famous for its own brand of locally brewed, springhouse-cooled dark beer. By the time we had visited three or four of these establishments we were in no condition to go on. So we picked a place to camp, which in our beer-benumbed state looked pretty good but turned out to be a peat bog, dry on the surface but wet enough beneath that we awoke the next morning to find our shiny new bikes sunk hub-deep in mud. An hour of furious effort got us back on the hardtop with the BMWs looking like veterans of an off-road rally—and their hung-over owners looking even worse.

For breakfast that morning we pulled into a little mountain *Gasthaus*, where crowds of friendly Bavarians gathered to admire with possessive pride the still-novel sight of post-war-model BMWs on German roads. The inn's portly proprietor ushered us with much bowing and scraping into his cool, dark dining room where we had to duck to avoid the huge sausages that hung from smoke-blackened beams. We sat by an open window listening to the sounds of a solitary woodchopper working in the hills beyond, and in due course our host reappeared, staggering under the weight of a ham and cheese omelet that must have taxed the resources of every farm in the village. This monstrous production, accompanied by jelly-slathered slabs of homemade bread and great, steaming mugs of coffee, banished what little of our hangovers we hadn't already sweated during our earlier escape from the swamp.

We went on to Starnberg in high spirits. There, the first person we met was a beautiful schoolteacher who would not be happy until she had been given a ride on a BMW. But because there was only one of her and two of us, we asked if she might not have an equally beautiful friend who was also pining for a ride. She allowed as how she did—"a blonde, very pretty, yah?" So while she went off to fetch this enchantress, Duncan and I argued over who was going to end up with whom. We had just resolved by the flip of a coin that I was to get the blonde, when our friend returned in company with a gargantuan, ugly Brunhilde.

We set off for the beach, reflecting on the maxim that a girl will rarely produce a blind date prettier than herself. To make matters worse, the engineers at BMW had not planned for the kind of load I was carrying, so I ground a good deal of metal off my new mufflers on the rough stone road.

Once at the beach my giant companion produced a vat of suntan lotion and, through a pantomime of grunts and giggles, indicated that I was to smear this stuff all over her back. I was already sick enough over the destruction of my mufflers, and the prospect of this job, which would have been like painting a barn, was

"Motorcycles," he said, "are like children, yah? You gif zem all ze best, und still sometimes zey go bad!"

In Venice, we rode around in gondolas and paid outrageous prices for beer.

too much. I told Duncan I'd meet him in Vienna and fled. He caught up with me an hour later, his girl having abandoned him in annoyance over my precipitous departure.

Our misfortunes in love were soon forgotten in the beauty of the country through which we were riding. We wound our way along twisting roads into the Alps, the bikes gasping a bit in the thinning air, and crossed over into Austria.

Duncan was not one to baby machinery. He flogged his bike hard right from the start, while I lagged way behind, dutifully following the break-in instructions to the letter. So it was all the more disappointing when, as we approached Vienna, my carefully maintained machine developed a howling bearing in the gearbox. Duncan had suffered enough over the years at my unflattering comments about his Horex to have no pity. He ragged me unmercifully as we searched through the labyrinthian streets of Vienna's industrial section trying to find BMW's factory-authorized mechanic. When at last we located this gentleman, we discovered that to be a mechanic in Austria is a far higher calling than it is here. The Master, clad in a spotless white coat, would not condescend to touch my machine until his assistants had entirely purified it from dirt. Then, before the admiring eyes of his apprentices, he fastidiously set to work, replacing the offending bearing without getting even a spot of oil on his jacket. He was immensely proud of BMWs and took it as a personal blow to his pride that mine should have failed me. "It is like children, yah? You gif zem all ze best, und still sometimes zey go bad!"

Our stay in Vienna passed in a happy haze of beer and Wiener Schnitzel. We would start each morning at the Cafe Mozart where, among the international collection of newspapers all carefully bound with split bamboo poles, we'd find the New York Times and read up on domestic events that seemed very far away. Then, as often as not, we would go our separate ways, meeting again in the evening to resume our pursuit of the ladies.

On one such day I set off by myself to find the Esterhazy Castle, where Haydn had been court composer. I got lost, as usual, and blundered instead onto the Hungarian border, where for the first time I saw the Iron Curtain. It was just that: two rows of electrified barbed wire with a mine field between them stretching off as far as the eye could see in both direc-

tions. There was a crater in the mine field and shreds of clothing hanging from the wire. From what I could gather, a Hungarian family tried to get across a few nights before. Only the son survived the mine explosion, and the Austrian authorities sent him back to his remaining relatives in Hungary. In retrospect, I think that particular day had a lot to do with my later decision to make a career of the Marine Corps.

Leaving Vienna, bound for Italy via Salzburg, Innsbruck and the Brenner Pass, we rode through the famous Vienna Woods and stopped in a wheat field to wait out a rain squall. While we watched from beneath a grove of pines, the sun broke through the clouds, flooding the fields below us with a golden light that was made all the more vivid by the rain-shrouded forest beyond. We stood, spellbound, as the sun came and went from behind wind-driven clouds, sending shimmering waves of light chasing shadows across the wheat, and witnessed the most beautiful moments of the summer.

The Brenner Pass provided an interesting contrast between precise Austrian bureaucrats on one side of the frontier and cheerful, bumbling Italian functionaries on the other. Once in Italy, however, we were received with surly scowls until we discovered that with our blond hair and BMW motorcycles, we were being mistaken for Germans. The memory of World War II was still very much alive in that part of the world, and there was plainly no love lost between the two former allies. Duncan somehow conjured up an American flag, which solved our problem.

Our first planned stop in Italy was Venice. There, as expected of tourists, we rode around in gondolas and paid outrageous prices for beer. But after the simple friendliness we had found in Austria, we felt uncomfortable enough in tourist-oriented Venice to cut short our stay and head inland for Padua and Veronna. In one of those ancient towns, I can no longer remember which, we went to an outdoor performance of *Aida* given in a still-intact Roman coliseum. Opera in Italy has none of the highbrow pretensions of the Metropolitan. For one thing, the audience can understand the words, so if a singer blows his lines, as often happened that night, there are hoots and jeers until the unfortunate performer starts over and gets it right. Vendors circulated through the stands, and at one point a tired old elephant that had been pressed into service from the local zoo for the Grand March disgraced itself on center stage. The crowd went wild while the chorus of Egyptian soldiers downed swords and upped shovels to clear away the steaming mountain.

During intermission, Duncan's injudicious remarks to a *senora* led to our being surrounded by an angry mob of hot-blooded gentlemen, all bent on defending the honor of the offended lady. After an uneasy couple of minutes it became plain enough that nobody really wanted to fight. Nonetheless, it seemed prudent not to stick around, so we climbed on the bikes and left as quietly as was possible, in view of the holes Brunhilde had worn in my mufflers.

From Padua we headed east again to Ravenna and then south along the Adriatic coast. We had by this time picked up another American, Gordon Fairburn, who was traveling through Europe with his guitar at a time before every American tourist carried a guitar. Gordon's singing earned us a lot of free meals. My singing did, too, although in my case, I'm sure that anguished music-lovers fed us in the hopes that I would eat rather than sing.

For lunch we usually had a loaf of bread, a hunk of cheese and a bottle of wine. I would eat most of the bread and cheese while Duncan and Gordon would drink most of the wine. Thus, Duncan's riding in the afternoon was sometimes a little shaky. Once, I was following him down a perfectly straight country road when, for no apparent reason, he, Gordon and the guitar shot off into a field of potatoes. I watched amazed as they churned along for some distance, throwing up a great roostertail of dirt and potatoes, before coming to rest unhurt but upside-down in a ditch.

This was one we couldn't fix. Duncan's headlight was squashed, shorting out the entire electrical system, and both carbs had inhaled bucketsful of mud. A crowd gathered from nowhere. Somebody produced a frayed piece of line that we had to buy at huge cost, and we set off again with Duncan in tow. We finally found a mechanic capable of jury-rigging a repair, then headed across the Appenine Mountains for Rome with a chastened Duncan swearing off the bottle as I have heard him do many times since.

Coming down the switchback roads off the Appenines, I practiced the art of countersteering through curves well enough to make for one of the fastest rides of my life. It was one of those unforgettable days when my bike and I became "one single moving part." The R50's acceleration was modest on flat ground, but more than adequate when assisted by gravity and a steep hill. With the folly of youth, I raced into each descending turn, leaning hard on the inboard handlebar to pitch the bike onto its ear, and ground my way around the corner in a shower of sparks. By racing standards, I don't suppose I was going all that fast, but in my mind's eye I saw myself flashing by Meier and Surtees and all the other Great Men of the age.

Instead, I flashed by a policeman tooling along on his bright red Moto Guzzi. "I've had it now," I thought, while hitting the brakes. Sure enough, I looked back to see the Guzzi in hot pursuit, and I started to pull over, wondering how the Marine Corps would take the news that I was languishing in an Italian jail. Instead, my mustachioed pursuer shot by, shouting "Avanti!" or whatever it is Italians shout when they want to race. So together we tore down the mountain, trading the lead back and forth as we went. At the bottom my opponent became once again a policeman and lectured me against speeding. I agreed to mend my ways, and he saluted solemnly before going off to resume his duties.

Approaching Rome we learned with chattering teeth that Caesar had not anticipated motorcycles when he paved his roads with cobblestones. In the city, we reverted once again to the uncomfortable role of tourists. At the Vatican we ran into some American girls we had earlier camped with on a moonlit Adriatic beach, but the stern presence of the Pope so stiffened their resolve against any additional lapses of virtue that we had no further comfort from that quarter. So we headed off for Pisa to climb the Leaning Tower in the company of a herd of urchins all trying to sell us souvenirs. There was no escape from these persistent entrepreneurs except through flight. So we rode back into the country, resolving over dinner to visit no more big cities until we arrived in France.

That night it rained. Our usual foul-weather plan when camping was to park the two bikes side-by-side and stretch a tarp between them to serve as a tent. We got this contrivance rigged just ahead of the downpour and were soon asleep beneath it. But as the night wore on, the tarp filled with enough water to tip the bikes over, Duncan's on him and mine on me. In our besotted state, we thought we were being attacked. Our frantic

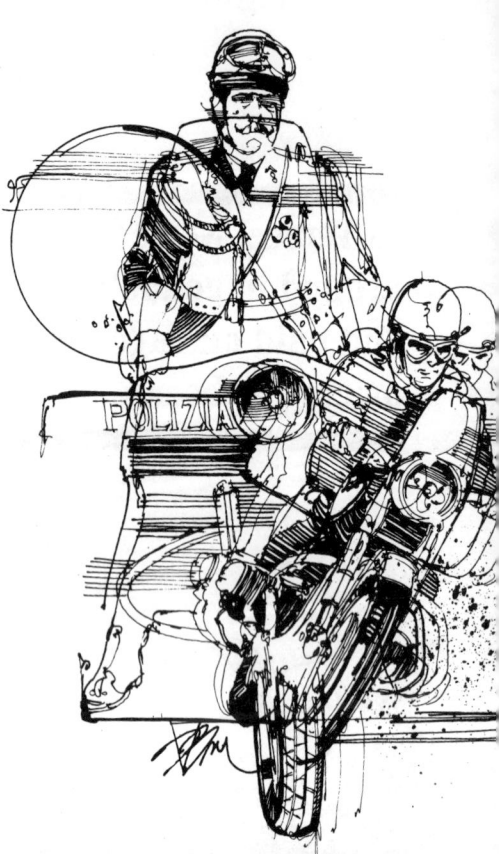

At the bottom of the hill, my opponent became once again a policeman.

struggles to get out from under our assailants only served to dump the remaining contents of the tarps on our heads. "Succuro!," bellowed Duncan. "The bastards are trying to drown us." Whereupon with the strength of desperation he hurled his machine clear and jumped to his feet. About this time I also got free from my bike and staggered upright, still under the tarp. Duncan spotted this strange, shrouded apparition and threw himself on what he took to be our attacker. It was my turn to holler "Succuro" as I floundered around, engulfed in canvas with Duncan flailing away outside.

By the time we got all this sorted out it was impossible to get back to sleep, so we rode all through the soggy night headed for what we hoped would be the fleshpots of the Italian Riviera. Instead, dawn revealed worn and dirty beaches, somehow looking all the more squalid in their early-morning emptiness. Disgusted, we turned northwest, back toward the mountains and the French

The tarp filled with enough water to tip the bikes over, and in our beer-besotted state we thought we were being attacked.

frontier. At the border town of Cottiennes we were tempted to linger by two beguiling sisters named Petri, but the summer was getting on and all of France, England and Scotland still lay ahead.

The long ride across the high, rolling hills of France's lovely Massif Central was one of the best of the summer. Today, the names on the map conjure up memories of magnificent meals—roast rabbit in Valence, truly memorable pastries in Le Puy, unforgettable wine everywhere. In Périgueux we ran afoul of *les gen-* *darmes* mounted on massive, prewar, flathead BMWs, but all ended well thanks to our mutual admiration for those machines. Then it was on to Bordeaux to stay with two splendid octogenarian ladies whose days were spent ministering to the elderly of their village, most of whom were 20 years younger than they were.

We crossed the English Channel at Cherbourg. First we went to Oxford, where Duncan was later to return as a student, and then into the English countryside. Riding on what for us was the wrong side of the road proved a bit of a trick, particularly at intersections, where we invariably looked left before proceeding into the path of furiously honking traffic.

In Scotland, the land of enchanted names, there were the towns of Ecclefechan, Lockerbie, Lesmahgow and then Glasgow, from whence Duncan's grandfather had left to seek his fortune in the New World. From Glasgow we continued north along the shore of Loch Lomond until Duncan hit wet oil and skidded into a pond. I was far enough behind to watch all this and was laughing so hard at the sight of him sitting disconsolately tank-deep in water that I hit the same patch and ended up right beside him. We drained everything, changed the oil in nearby Arrochar and were off again, the bulletproof BMWs apparently none the worse for their dunking.

The road from Arrochar led through Crianlarich and Daimally to Oban where we rode with a boatload of sheep across the Firth of Lorn to the Isle of Mull. Duncan had stayed on Mull as a boy. His old friend Neal the Gamekeeper still lived in the same thatch-roof cottage, surrounded by the guns and fly rods that were the tools of his trade. Neal walked with a limp he had picked up as a dispatch rider for the British in North Africa. As he told the story, days of artillery fire had so stirred up the desert sand that the only way he could find his way between positions was to loop the wire that ran between command posts over his footpeg and follow it blindly to his destination. This technique worked well enough until one day he met another rider doing the same thing from the opposite direction. The resulting crash put him out of the war.

Hanging over us like a dark cloud was the knowledge that time was running out for our European odyssey. I had to get to Quantico and Duncan back to Yale. With the sense that something never to be repeated was about to end, we rode back to Glasgow where we arranged to have the bikes shipped home before flying out for New York.

I kept that old R50 until a mine explosion in Viet Nam ended my Marine Corps career and, I thought, my career as a motorcyclist as well. But a couple of years ago I succumbed to nostalgia and bought another BMW. I don't ride it much, but when I do I always look in my mirror for that policeman's red Moto Guzzi, and I think back on distant rides when the whole world still seemed to lie along the road ahead. ◙

BMW K75
FOUR MINUS ONE EQUALS K75

BMW's CONCEPT FOR ITS NEW K75 is nothing if not audacious: Take a successful four-cylinder motorcycle, chop one cylinder from its engine, and then stuff the resulting smaller-displacement Triple back into the Four's chassis.

In this way, the new K75 expands the BMW range, but can it be taken seriously? After all, would Yamaha create an FZ560 by lopping one cylinder off of the FZ750 and recycling the 750 frame? Or Honda a VF750R V-Three version of the VF1000R?

Regardless of how other manufacturers might feel, BMW takes this idea seriously indeed. From the very beginning of the K program, BMW planned to produce both the four-cylinder K100 *and* the three-cylinder K75. Only a marketing decision dictated that the K100 got released first.

And make no mistake: The K75 really is the K100 minus its front cylinder, with only a few additional changes. First is engine tune; instead of the 67.5 bhp that might be expected from three-fourths of a 90-horse K100, the K75 produces 75 bhp. This power boost is through straightforward means. The K75's cam timing is longer, and its compression ratio is up to 11.0:1 from 10.2:1 on the K100. The result is more peak power per cubic centimeter than on the K100, although with correspondingly less mid-range.

Aside from engine tune, the other major difference between the two engines is the addition of a balance shaft to the K75. Because the Three was always a planned addition to the line, provision for this balancer was made in the original design. The shaft that drives the clutch and water pump was designed so it could be transformed into a balance shaft by adding counterweights; the 1-to-1 speed ratio between crank and shaft was already correct. With the weighted shaft, the K75 is smoother than its four-cylinder parent.

These engine dissimilarities are almost the only real differences between the K75 and the K100; any chassis changes are minimal. The K100 frame is retained on the K75, with only the angle of the front downtubes and the location of the front engine mounts altered to accommodate the shorter engine. Wheelbase, steering geometry and seat height are unchanged. Because the smaller engine requires less cooling capacity, the K75 uses a smaller radiator; and the narrower radiator shroud mates to a slightly sleeker gas tank that is marginally smaller than the K100's. The biggest visual difference between Ks is the airspace between front tire and engine—and, on the K75C, the handlebar fairing that is standard.

The other K75 model, the K75S, is distinguished by the sportiest fairing in the entire K lineup. This small, frame-mounted fairing will surely give less protection than the K100RS fairing, but BMW claims less drag as well, with a claimed top speed of 128

K75S uses a small, frame-mounted fairing that offers less rider-protection than the K100RS fairing, but the K75 has less frontal area and reduced drag.

The crankshaft on the K75 is a 120-degree design. Balance weights added to the water-pump drive shaft eliminate typical three-cylinder vibration.

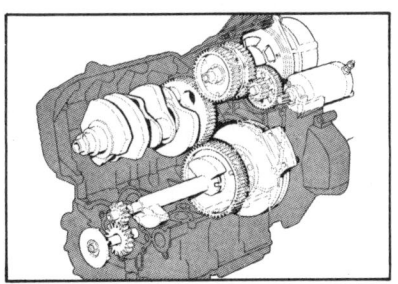

The two new K75 models, the S and the C, round out the line and bring the total of K-series BMWs to five.

Fairing on the K75S is narrow and sporty, favoring aerodynamics over rider protection. Instruments and controls are identical to the K100's.

The K75C's standard equipment includes a small handlebar fairing and a pricetag that makes it the least-expensive K-series BMW.

mph, only six mph less than claimed for the K100RS.

Considering all of the design and visual similarities between K100 and K75, a ride on both offers quite a surprise: They don't *feel* that similar. The K75's engine is noticeably smoother, and its three cylinders provide a less busy feel. Gear whine is the loudest mechanical noise coming from the engine, and the exhaust note has been silenced to the point where the three-cylinder howl is undistinguished.

Neither is the Three all that much slower than the Four; it makes less power, but that's partially offset by a lower final-drive ratio and 20 pounds less weight. The smoother engine also encourages use of higher rpm; on a twisty road, the K75 might be run in a lower gear, when, under the same conditions, the temptation would be to upshift the K100. And while the Four has a slight performance edge, the Three is the more pleasant engine to live with.

Handling is equally disparate. If the K75C is 20 pounds lighter than a K100, the steering feels as if every one of those 20 pounds came off the front wheel. Steering effort is sharply reduced, and only a slight pressure on the handlebar rolls the Three into a turn. The steering is so light at low speeds on the wide-bar-equipped K75C that, initially, there's a tendency to overcontrol. The handling is quite good overall, though, considering that this is a softly suspended, shaft-drive bike with a touring orientation. As it's pushed toward the limit, it can misbehave by weaving in over-90-mph corners, and the front tire sometimes runs out of traction before the rear. Still, under most conditions, the K75 can sustain a very quick pace without straining its rider.

On the highway, the small fairing of the K75C is effective in breaking the wind on the chest without creating enough turbulence to rattle a helmet visor, and the engine hums along smoothly at just over 4200 rpm

at 60 mph. Unlike K100s we have tested, the K75 doesn't buzz its footpegs at these speeds. Above 6500 rpm in top gear, there is some vibration, but it's not intrusive. Ten-hour days on this motorcycle are completely reasonable.

Actually, reasonable may be the best word to describe both K75s, the C and the S. Both offer acceptable, albeit not stunning, performance, at a lesser price than their four-cylinder relatives. If German prices are any indication, the K75C will sell for slightly more than $5000, compared to about $6000 for a 1985 K100; and the K75S will go for about $6000, against $7200 for the 1985 K100RS. That makes the Triples particularly attractive compared to the Fours, for under most conditions, the K75 is the more enjoyable motorcycle.

With results like that to use as an example, perhaps it's the other manufacturers who should be considering the merits of cylinder subtraction.

—*Steve Anderson*

BMW K75C

WHEN THE RIDE MATTERS

GERMANS HAVE A PARTICU-larly strong idea of what a motorcycle should be, and an even stronger idea of what a motorcycle *shouldn't* be. A motorcycle should be something for riding, touring and enjoying, not merely for racing, profiling and showing off. A motorcycle should be simple, strong and light, not glitzy, complex and loaded with gadgets. A motorcycle should be . . . well, something very much like BMW's K75.

But then, the K75 is more than just a German ideal given three dimensions: it's a motorcycle dedicated to the act of motorcycle riding.

You get that message with your first glance at the bike. You see no racy color schemes or clip-on handlebars, because things like that would be just as much out of place as a teardrop tank and a high-rise handlebar. The K75 isn't striving for a flashy image and it isn't supposed to remind you of anything but what it is—a no-nonsense road bike. The footpegs are where footpegs should be on a road bike, not where they should be on Freddie Spencer's GP racer. The handlebar is shaped so it's comfortable for hours of riding on the road, not just for a few minutes of sitting in the showroom. The engine was designed for realistic road performance, not for ultimate dragstrip numbers.

A ride on the BMW drives the point home even further. Like many European streetbikes, the K75 has an affinity for speed, becoming increasingly comfortable as the speedometer needle climbs. The handlebar is quite narrow, almost flat and kind of far forward, positioning your upper body so that it tucks in, under the wind; but you're still not in the typical wrist-punishing sport-racer posture. And the relatively low and forward footpeg position is more touring-like than sportbike-typical. The pegs are just high enough to keep ground clearance from being a realistic problem, but not so high that they make you feel cramped on a long ride. The resultant riding position is excellent for practically any type of riding. Actually, the K75 is more comfortable than just about any bike currently on the market, short of a full-size American-style touring rig.

But what gives the K75 most of its air of German practicality is its liquid-cooled, six-valve, dohc engine. The power range is so broad that it's hard to know what rpm the engine is turning without looking at the tach. But it doesn't matter; the engine always seems to pull, regardless. When going through a turn, you can shift now, you can shift later, or you don't have to shift at all. The K75 has a torque curve that is as broad as that of most literbikes.

This 750cc BMW won't set any speed records, though, not with its claimed 75 horses. But it's BMW's philosophy that a motorcycle doesn't *have* to produce enough power to spin the earth on its axis, that a bike should have only as much power as it needs—no more, no less. And that's precisely what the K75 has.

That same kind of Teutonic logic seemed to dictate the way the rest of the bike was built, too. BMW did just what was necessary to produce the 750, without waste, without extravagance. The engine is, for all intents and purposes, a four-cylinder, 987cc K100 engine with one cylinder—and its 247cc of displacement—lopped off the front. The result is a 740cc Triple.

Some might call that cheap and easy engineering, not logical and functional; but this simply isn't the case, because both the three-cylinder K75 and the four-cylinder K100 were designed and developed simultaneously. BMW was, after all, already making one radical move by departing from the traditional boxer Twin. To expect dealers and customers to have a positive reaction to *two* completely new and different designs would not have been realistic. Besides, BMW claims that 80 percent of the K75's parts are interchangeable with the latest K100's. That *is* logical and functional.

Which is not to say that there are no differences between the two motorcycles other than cylinder count.

For one, the K75 uses a gear-driven counterbalancer running parallel to the crankshaft. It smoothes the vibrations that arise due to the the rocking-couple produced by the K75's three-throw, 120-degree crankshaft. The K75 also makes more horsepower per cubic centimeter than its K100 big brother, a feat accomplished through a higher compression ratio (11:1 on the K75, compared with 10.2:1 on the K100), redesigned combustion chambers, shorter intake manifolds and different exhaust-system tuning.

Other technical aspects of the K75 are common with the K100. Both have Bosch electronic fuel injection, and both engines drive through a dry clutch, a five-speed transmission and a shaft final drive. The K75's final-drive ratio is slightly lower (higher numerically) than the K100's, but the rear end of the motorcycle has the same unique swingarm arrangement as the K100. A single shock, sans linkage, mounts only to one side of the swingarm, simply because there *is* only one side of the swingarm. The massive, cast-aluminum driveshaft housing is the only structural member connecting the rear wheel to the motorcycle. This arrangement is very strong, and it makes rear-wheel removal ridiculously easy.

With the K75 having so much in common with the K100, BMW felt it was important to add a few touches here and there that would give the 750 its own identity. Most are subtle—such as the shape of the 3-into-1 exhaust system's muffler, which is triangular on the Triple rather than square as on the Four. The K75 has a narrower radiator, as well, which makes the whole bike seem thinner

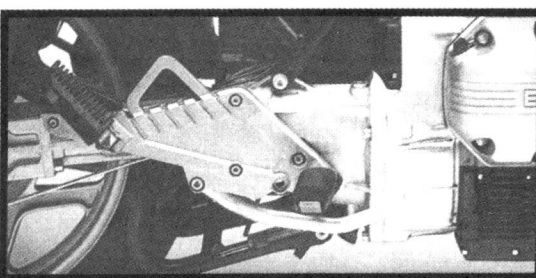

The passenger footpeg bracket actually doubles as a convenient footrest when you pull your toes up for full-tilt cornering.

than the K100. And there also is a small, fork-mounted fairing that will appear only on the K75C model. The touring-oriented K75T comes with a taller windscreen, and the sporty K75S, to be announced later in the year, will have a frame-mounted fairing. None of the three fairings was lifted from the K100, but instead were designed to give the Triple a look all its own.

Still, the K75 could easily pass for a K100 in the eyes of anyone who isn't paying much attention. But if you ride both bikes, there's no danger of confusing the two. The K75 has the unique exhaust drone produced only by a 120-degree Triple, whereas the K100 sounds like a typical four-cylinder UJM. And unlike the K100, the K75 is dead-smooth. At low revs, high revs and everything between, the Triple glides along so smoothly that it could just be coasting downhill with the key turned off. There's no

hint of the left-footpeg vibration that loosened the toenails of most early K100 riders. In fact, the K75 will hold its own against any bike when it comes to engine smoothness. The only time the rider is aware of any vibration at all is on trailing throttle, when the engine reminds him of its presence with a very light, low-frequency buzzing.

If you're still not sure which is the 1000 and which is the 750, any twisty road can show you the light. Even though the weight difference is only around 20 pounds, the Triple feels much smaller and lighter. It still isn't what you would call exceptionally light-handling, but only because Japan's featherweight Fours with their 16-inch front wheels have set new standards of agility. In true German fashion, however, the K75 steers quickly enough to get the job done, no matter how tight the road.

Working into a smooth and easy

rhythm on a snaky road is no problem for the BMW. Cornering is natural and easy, thanks to the bike's omnipresent power, neutral steering and the sticky Pirelli Phantom tires that came on our test bike (K75s will also be delivered with Continentals, Metzelers and Michelins). And perhaps the biggest contributor to the K75's cooperative handling is the exceptionally low center of gravity provided by the laid-down engine.

But the harder the pace, the easier it is to find the BMW's handling limits. While the twin front disc brakes are fine around town, they just aren't up to super-hard charges on back roads. When you dive into a turn a little too deep, a one- or two-finger squeeze won't cut it; instead, the front brake wants your whole *hand* on the lever. Then, once your knuckles have turned sufficiently white to slow the Beemer down, fork dive is the next annoyance, for the front end is too soft for serious cut-and-thrust sportbiking antics. The rear suspension is a better compromise between freeway and back-route travel. The springing and damping strike an excellent balance to create a ride that's always smooth and predictable.

But all is not perfect at the rear end, either, for it is there, in the shaft final drive, where you will find the K75C's single most annoying trait: torque reaction by the chassis, a characteristic that has almost become a BMW trademark. Practically every time you upshift or open the throttle very quickly, the entire bike raises up on its suspension; snapping the throttle closed causes the bike to squat down on its fork and shock. A sudden blip of the gas can cause the bike to jump up so violently that it feels like the rear wheel has come off the ground. This chassis behavior, longtime Beemerphiles will say, is something you can get used to. But in this day and age of motorcycle sophistication, you shouldn't have to "get used to" anything.

But then, K75 owners *won't* have to get used to the cramped riding positions, the bothersome engine vibrations, the all-or-nothing powerbands and the overall impracticality prevalent in so many modern motorcycles. That's a more-than-fair trade-off, especially in view of the K75C's list price of $4700. For that, you get a very German motorcycle at a very Japanese price. You don't get much in the way of frills or exotic images, only what's necessary for the ride.

That's the German way. And after a ride on a K75, you just might believe that it's the right way. ◙

BMW finally has abandoned its rock-hard "ergonomic" grips in favor of closed-cell foam grips similar to BMX and aftermarket items sold in the U.S. The grips still aren't everyone's favorite, but they're a big improvement.

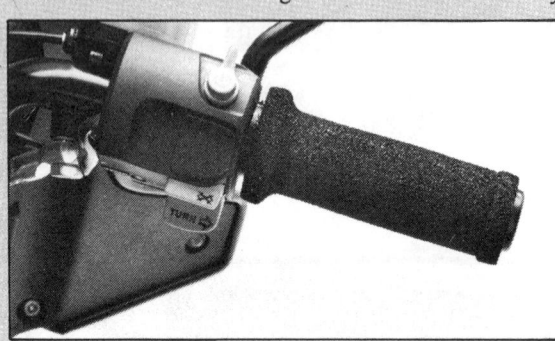

Our test bike came with BMW's detachable touring saddlebags, but they're not standard equipment. The bags and their mounting brackets tack $311 onto the K75C's $4700 base price.

BMW K75C

SPECIFICATIONS

GENERAL

List price	$4700
as tested	$5011
Importer	BMW of North America BMW Plaza Montvale, NJ 07645
Customer service phone	(201) 573-2151
Warranty	3 yr./unlimited mi.

CHASSIS

Weight as tested:	
Tank empty	494 lb.
Tank full	528 lb.
Weight distribution, front/rear, percent:	
Tank empty	4.29/57.1
Tank full	43.9/56.1
Fuel capacity	5.6 gal.
Wheelbase	60.6 in.
Rake/trail	27.5°/3.9 in.
Handlebar width	25.5 in.
Seat height	32.0 in.
Ground clearance	6.9 in.
GVWR	992 lb.
Load capacity (tank full)	464 lb.

DRIVETRAIN

Engine	liquid-cooled, four-stroke, inline-Four
Bore x stroke	67.0 x 70.0mm
Displacement	740.0cc
Compression ratio	11.0:1
Claimed power	75 bhp @ 8500 rpm
Claimed torque	50 ft.-lb. @ 6750 rpm
Valve train	dohc, two valves per cyl., shim adjustment
Valve adjustment intervals	5000 mi.
Carburetion	fuel injection
Air filter	dry paper
Lubrication	wet sump
Oil capacity	4.0 qt.
Starter	electric
Primary drive	straight-cut gear
Clutch	single-plate, dry
Final drive	shaft
Gear ratios, overall:1	
1st	14.40
2nd	9.47
3rd	7.36
4th	6.02
5th	5.34

ELECTRICAL

Electrical power	460w
Battery	12v/20ah
Headlight	55/60w, halogen

SUSPENSION/TIRES/BRAKES

Front suspension:	
Manufacturer	Fichtel & Sachs
Tube diameter	41.5mm
Wheel travel	6.8 in.
Adjustments	none
Rear suspension:	
Manufacturer	Boge
Type	single-shock
Wheel travel	3.9 in.
Adjustments	spring preload
Wheels:	
Front	MT 2.50 x 18
Rear	MT 2.75 x 18
Tires:	
Front	100/90H18 Pirelli Phantom
Rear	120/90H18 Pirelli Phantom
Rear tire revs. per mi.	778
Brakes:	
Front	(2) 11.2 in. disc
Rear	7.9 in. disc

PERFORMANCE

ACCELERATION

Time to distance:	
¼ mi.	13.38 sec. @ 98.46 mph
Time to speed, sec.	
0–30 mph	1.6
0–40 mph	2.4
0–50 mph	3.4
0–60 mph	4.4
0–70 mph	5.9
0–80 mph	7.8
0–90 mph	10.1
Top gear time to speed, sec.	
40–60 mph	5.7
60–80 mph	5.3

SPEED IN GEARS

Measured top speed	110 mph
Calculated at 8250 rpm redline:	
1st gear	44 mph
2nd gear	67 mph
3rd gear	87 mph
4th gear	106 mph
5th gear	119 mph
Engine speed at 60 mph	4160 rpm

FUEL MILEAGE

High/low/avg.	60/38/46 mpg
Avg. range inc. reserve	258 mi.

BRAKING DISTANCE

from 30 mph	35 ft.
from 60 mph	128 ft.

SPEEDOMETER ERROR

30 mph indicated	30 mph
60 mph indicated	60 mph

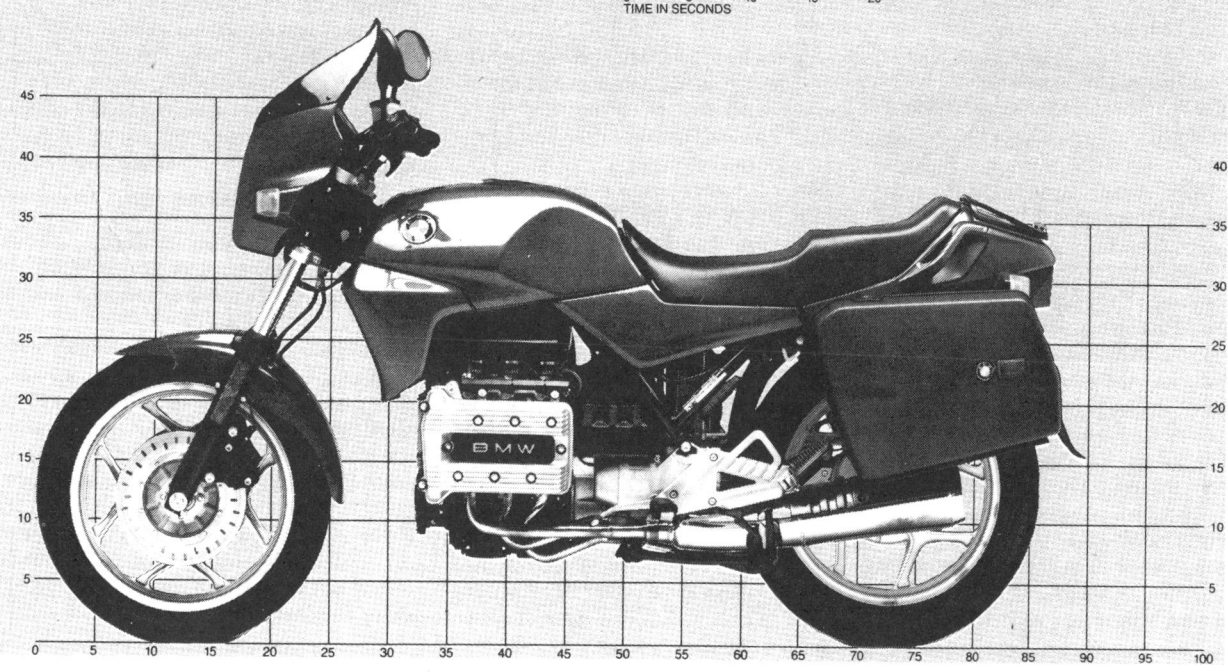

Does a sporting BMW ever stop being a touring bike?

IT TOOK NEARLY A YEAR. FIRST came the K75C, then the K75T, and now, finally, the K75S. With it, BMW's K75 model line is complete. And according to BMW, this new S-model is targeted as a pure sportbike, while the C-model K75 is designed as a sport-tourer and the T is the standard model.

Fortunately for BMW, its engineers didn't have to make many changes to the basic K75C design when isolating the sporting elements from the touring. That was possible because the K75C was already well on its way to being a good sportbike.

Among the many things the K75S and K75C have in common is the engine. Both use the same fuel-injected, counterbalanced, 740cc inline-Three, and so both also produce the same smooth, seemingly endless powerband. They also share the same frame and unique, single-sided swingarm. In addition, much of the bodywork is the same on the C and S models, although the S has a completely new, frame-mounted fairing with an added lower cowling.

That three-quarter fairing does a nice job of keeping excessive amounts of wind blast from assaulting the rider; but at the same time, it allows enough wind to hit the rider's chest and shoulders to help support

his upper-body weight at speed. This is important to the S-model's comfort, because its lower, narrower handlebar tucks the rider more into a true sportbike position than does the wider, higher bar on the K75C.

By far, however, the most significant difference between the K75S and the other K75 models is in the suspension. The front fork in particular is new, and it makes the S-model feel like a considerably different motorcycle. While the K75C has almost seven inches of softly sprung, lightly damped front-wheel travel, the S comes with just over five inches of travel controlled by stiffer springing and rebound damping.

These changes mean that the infamous BMW front-end dive is greatly reduced on the K75S. In fact, until braking goes beyond the moderate, the S-bike's front end has a taut, sensitive feel more like what you might expect from Japanese sportbikes than from anything produced by BMW in recent years. Yet, in spite of the stiffer front fork, the ride remains smooth and compliant over a wide variety of road surfaces.

To balance the suspension, BMW equipped the K75S's single rear shock with a stiffer spring. While that change provides an overall improvement over the K75C's rear suspen-

sion and reduces the drive-shaft torque-reaction somewhat, the stiffer spring overpowers the damping, allowing the shock to top-out with surprising regularity. In fact, both the fork and the shock could benefit from more rebound damping.

Still, the K75S makes light work of fast, sweeping corners, especially those that do not require super-hard braking going in, or maximum acceleration coming out. Rather, this is a bike that rewards smoothness in the twisties. So it's best—and on the K75S, easy—to settle into a fast, silky rhythm on back roads. When the corners get tight or an "S" curve crops up in a fast section, however, the narrow handlebar forces the rider to work noticeably harder.

But all things considered, the K75S seems to be a reasonable, enjoyable sporting machine, even though its $5950 price tag ($500 more than the K75C) puts it at the high end of the 750cc class. But for that price, you get a sportbike that's comfortable and easy to ride over long distances—and one that can be equipped with the mounting bracketry and detachable luggage from the K75C. Which just goes to show that no matter how much "sport" you put into a BMW, you can never really get all of the "touring" out of it.